IN THE FOOTSTEPS OF THE CAMEL

IN THE FOOTSTEPS OF THE CAMEL

A Portrait of The Bedouins of Eastern Saudi Arabia in Mid-Century

Text and photographs by
Eleanor Nicholson

Foreword by
H.H. Amir Abdul Mohsin Ibn Jalawi

TRANSWORLD ARABIAN LIBRARY
RIYADH

STACEY INTERNATIONAL
LONDON

SECTION OF THE EASTERN PROVINCE, KINGDOM OF SAUDI ARABIA, IN THE EARLY 1960s

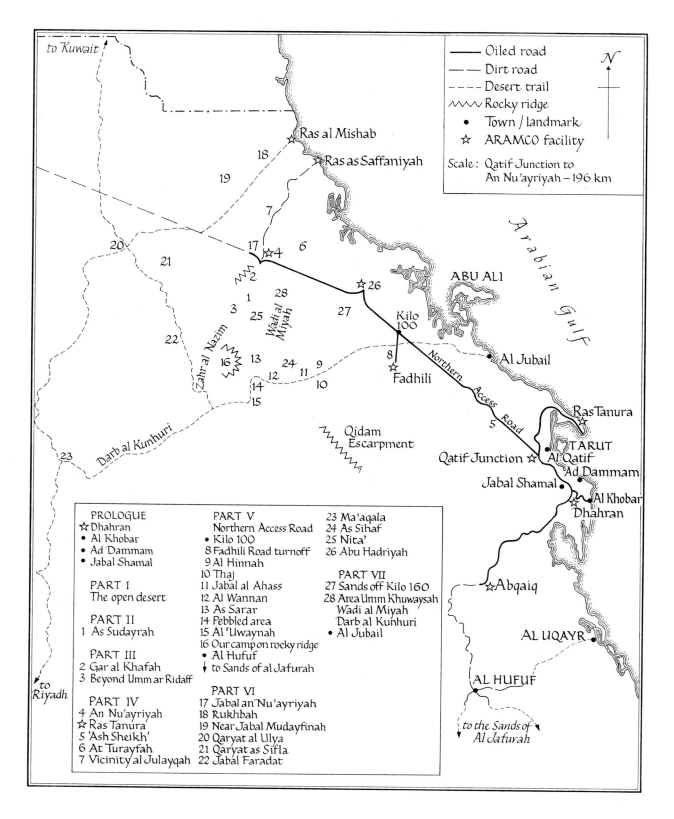

to Kuwait

Oiled road
Dirt road
Desert trail
Rocky ridge
Town / landmark
ARAMCO facility

Scale : Qatif Junction to
An Nu'ayriyah – 196 km

N

Ras al Mishab
Ras as Saffaniyah

Arabian Gulf

ABU ALI

Al Jubail

Kilo 100

Fadhili

Ras Tanura

Northern Access Road

Qidam Escarpment

Qatif Junction

TARUT
Al Qatif
Ad Dammam

Jabal Shamal

Al Khobar
Dhahran

Abqaiq

AL UQAYR

AL HUFUF

to the Sands of Al Jafurah

Zahr al Nazim

Wadi al Miyah

Darb al Kunhuri

to Riyadh

Dedication
To Russ—Linda—and Cynthia, who are the true authors of this book along with those formative days of the Kingdom of Saudi Arabia—the '50s and '60s— in which we all shared.

Editor
Charlotte Breese

Editorial Assistant
Sydney Francis

Design
John Fitzmaurice
Keith Savage

Cartographer
Reginald Piggott

IN THE FOOTSTEPS OF THE CAMEL
published by Stacey International
128 Kensington Church Street, London W8 4BH
Telex: 298768 STACEY G

Set in Monophoto Photina by
SX Composing Limited, Essex, England

Printed and bound by
Butler and Tanner, 35 Headfort Place, London SW1

Note
For readers who are not familiar with the
complexities of the Arabic language, Arabic words
appear in the text in italics and plurals are
included in the singular form expressed.

Author's Acknowledgments
My sincere thanks go to officials of the Ministry of
Information, Riyadh, Kingdom of Saudi Arabia,
who with pride in their heritage approved the
publication of the historic photographs presented
in this book. In particular, I wish to thank Mr
Abdur Rahman ar Rashid, Mr Misfer S. al Misfer,
and Mr Fahd al Hajri of Riyadh, and Dr S. Jimjoon
of Jeddah.

I gratefully acknowledge an indebtedness to
my consultant, Sheikh Mohammed Almana,
authority on Bedouin life and the days of Ibn Saud.
His personal help and guidance were invaluable.

It was Mr Jaber Jum'ah of Al Khobar, Saudi
Arabia, General Supervisor of Publications for the
Arabian American Oil Company, who generously
sought out and translated the series of traditional
verses interspersed throughout the book. I also
thank him for the first inkling into the derivation
of chants repeated during the performance of the
Ardah, the national dance.

Appreciation goes to the Arabian American
Oil Company for the security of its early rescue
system should we have become stranded in the
desert, and for the use of its unique documents and
out-of-print books contained in the former
Arabian Research Library.

My youthful days at Scripps College, Claremont,
California, have a bearing on this book, for there I
became initiated into the Humanities that set me
on the road to adventure and to understanding
of the Ancient World.

Perhaps having someone believe in you is the
most important feature of all. For this, my
warmest thanks go to Fawzia Jalawi, wife of
H. H. Amir Abdul Mohsin Ibn Jalawi, Governor of
the Eastern Province, as well as daughter-in-law
of that great desert warrior Abdullah Ibn Jalawi.

No list of acknowledgments for an author's
first effort would be complete without mentioning
the patience, encouragement and advice of family
and friends, nor gratefully giving recognition to
the professional guidance of Stacey International
experts who turned a manuscript into a book.

CONTENTS

FOREWORD

During the 1950s, many westerners came to live in the Eastern Province, among them the author, whose book reveals a need to reach out in search of a kinship with our people. Her expressed love for the vast desert areas equals our own, and the related personal encounters between her family and Bedouin tribes are fascinating and absorbing. Historical researchers seeking additional documentation on the Bedu will find in this book an intimate view of family life, as seen through the eyes of a perceptive foreigner.

Eleanor Nicholson's unusual photographs reflect sincerity and respect for a lifestyle so different from her own and constitute a valuable addition to our understanding of desert existence during a particular period of time. One senses in them a stimulus for enriched relationships between peoples of the world.

It is important to note, however, that since the events related by the author, great industrial and technological advancements have taken place in the Kingdom. Many Bedu have moved to the towns and onto farms. The Government has not overlooked the needs of those Bedouins who choose to live the traditional life of the desert. Improved roads and dug wells allow for easier travel and access to clean water. Supplies are plentiful in the villages. Families take their children to school and seek health care at Government clinics. Many purchase cars, and the Toyota pickup truck bouncing across the desert has become the trademark of today.

The traditional standards that make Bedouin culture unique have not changed with less rigorous demands. That great spirit of hospitality, generosity, honor and faith—attested to by the author—remains paramount in every *bait ash sha'ar*.

H.H. Amir Abdul Mohsin Ibn Jalawi
Governor of the Eastern Province
Dammam, Kingdom of Saudi Arabia
February 2, 1983

INTRODUCTION
The Bedouin—Prince of the Desert

The term Bedouin means people of the desert. Wandering tribes have existed in many areas of the world, but the Bedouin of the Arabian Peninsula produced a culture complete in itself, and as timeless as the desert that influenced it.

His environment brought forth qualities of great human value: an intense love of freedom and a sense of equality with all men. Pride and an aristocratic bearing stemmed from a lineage he could trace back to Ismael, son of Abraham. He gave allegiance to no man, clung to his proud free existence and feared only God.

Group solidarity was vital. Thus, he lived in tribes and sub-tribes, his leaders chosen from among those most qualified and not necessarily by right of descent. The family was paramount and individual conduct essential to tribal survival. An act of disgrace degraded the tribe, and punishments were severe, for reparation of honor was imperative. Judgment lay in the hands of the *ulema*, the religious authority who interpret and apply the Sharia, the law of Islam revealed in the Koran, Holy Book of Islam. Courage, generosity, hospitality, preservation of pure blood lines, and honor were attributes that strengthened the group.

The harshness of his desert inspired in the Bedouin a fervent devoutness to God, as well as a classic purity of language. He developed a poetry of expression born of loneliness, as he contemplated blackest nights bursting with stars, and the infinity that surrounded him.

His style of life engendered a complete inner security, and he envied no man. It gave to his women an unsophisticated charm and a simple approach to each day. Throughout the centuries, the women worked and fought side by side with their men, demanding reparation of honor and victory in battle. The clothes they wore reflected the austerity of life, the need for protection from their environment, and the demands of the moral codes. Physical hardships seemed all worthwhile in the glow of a campfire, in the birth of human and animal offspring—all "daughters of the tent"—and in the freedom of existence.

Before the unification of the Kingdom of Saudi Arabia, fighting was a way of life. The Bedouin raided his neighbor in an aura of chivalry, though there were times when he resorted to brutality and treachery. Fewer in number the Bedouin may be today, but he still exercises his moral codes and performs five daily prayers to Allah. His senses respond to the call of the wind, to the promise of rains, to the searing heat of summer and to the uplifting voice of Islam.

In 1950 it was estimated the nomads comprised approximately one-third of the population of the Arabian Peninsula. In 1974, at the time of the first complete census taken in Saudi Arabia, the unsettled population of the Kingdom had shrunk to little more than one-fourth. Today, approximately one-tenth of the population still leads a nomadic existence—a reduction due to the Government's efforts to encourage the Bedouin to settle and to farm the land. But, if his numbers have diminished, his culture has not.

To try to share this life style of the Bedouin— so distant from our own—was an experience at once humbling, awesome, delightful and inspiring. Our family came to love this Prince of the Desert and his family, to enjoy his sense of humor, to admire his strength of will and to feel not a little guilty for the Western influence we represented that was encroaching upon his centuries-old way of life.
The Author
November 1982
Madinat Al Jubail Al Sinaiyah

PROLOGUE

The "prop" flight from London had been long and wearisome. Deplaned at last on the shores of the United States, fatigued travelers milled through the Customs Hall, intent on clearing luggage. No one noticed a huge Stars and Stripes that draped in silken splendor along a tall staff positioned near the exit doors. No one, that is, except a small girl.

Bored of waiting with her family amid mounds of luggage, the child slipped past uniformed guards and swung under a brass railing, as polished as the staff itself. She hung onto her bag of Pan Am blue and stood on tiptoes to finger the glittering fringe edging the bottom stripe of red. Her loud voice resounded through the hall.

"I know about this flag — it belongs to the King!"

The place was U.S. Customs, Idylwild International Airport, New York. The year was 1959. And the child was mine! After two months of airplanes and European hotels, Cyndy had found something she could relate to—a flag. No matter that Old Glory of the United States of America didn't have a field of deep green with an unsheathed sword embroidered in white—the emblem of her "homeland".

I hoped no one noticed this diminutive American citizen who accepted the sovereignty of a king, but when our family stood its turn at the inspection bench, the Customs Officer smiled at her and said, "Welcome home!".

Home! The United States I had left nine years before, and where our family now returned on vacation from residence in the Middle East. Five-year-old Cynthia, and her sister Linda, aged seven, looked on the United States as just another foreign country where they visited Grandma in California, as they would the Louvre in Paris, or the koala bears in Australia. "Home" to our daughters was the Kingdom of Saudi Arabia, that eternity of desert lying between the Red Sea and the Arabian Gulf. Here they were born and went to school, celebrated Muslim holidays, rode Arabian mares over low dunes and lived in an American compound encircled by a high perimeter fence. Home, more accurately, consisted of the Americanized Middle Eastern operating areas of ARAMCO, the Arabian American Oil Company.

In February 1950, I had resigned my job at Paramount Pictures, Inc., in Hollywood, California, and boarded a TWA Ambassador flight for the Kingdom of Saudi Arabia, where I would join my husband Russ who was employed by ARAMCO. Arriving there convinced me I had merely exchanged one world of make-believe for another. Bedouin caravans crept across the sands, rounding the base of Jabal Shamal on their way to the fishing village of Dammam. Plumed litters swayed on the backs of camels, and cloaked and masked women appeared wardrobed for a de Mille epic of Biblical vintage. I waited for a director to shout "Cut!", but of course he never did. The scene I watched was real.

My early days in Dhahran, headquarters town of ARAMCO, revolved around the local needs of an expatriate community. Running a "Brownie Troop", and sewing at "Amy's" for Palestinian Relief did not fill a growing void, nor prevent the perimeter fence from closing in. I needed to touch, to understand this kingdom where I had come to live, but my own culture was as much a barrier as the customs of Muslim society.

Al Khobar on the Gulf was the closest native village to Dhahran. Sometimes we caught sight of Saudi women on the streets, veiled in long cloaks of black, but our presence only prompted them to hurry away. Invitations to the homes of Saudi employees did not include a visit to the family women, isolated in their own apartments. Muslim custom does not provide for social mixing of the sexes. Sightseeing trips were few and closely supervised to prevent incidents between cultures. In his wisdom, King Ibn Saud hoped to prevent western technology from crashing down on the ancient villages of the Eastern Province where we lived. He also let it be known that ARAMCO employees were in the Kingdom at his personal invitation and were accorded the status of Guests of the King.

In time, the birth of one daughter and then a second assuaged the feeling that I had no identity in this Kingdom and that my own world—now half the globe away—went on without me.

In 1956 we took up residence in the lovely seaside "refinery" town of Ras Tanura, about fifty miles north of Dhahran on the Gulf. Here sour crude was processed into sweet and piped into tankers berthed at terminal pier. By 1960, our original two year stay had stretched to ten, and my need to feel kinship with the Kingdom was still there.

Periodically, the USS *Laffey* or *Duxberry Bay* tied up at the Ras Tanura Port during visits to the Arabian Gulf. On such occasions, I pointed out to our daughters the true significance of the Stars and Stripes flying from the destroyer's stern, hoping to arouse a feeling for their citizenship. We always invited some of the men for dinner and cheered the Navy Team at donkey-baseball games. I was pleased to observe their interest in these blue-jacketed seamen, until I discovered it was only the sailor hats they were after!

"The United States is your country, not ours," Linda declared. "Our home is Arabia."

Respect for their feelings awakened a determination to find the true Arabia—not the ARAMCO communities, unrealistic bits of oil-town America set on the fringes of impenetrable deserts. The Kingdom meant the historical capital city of Riyadh, high on the plateau of the Najd. It was Makkah, the holy city, sacred to millions of Muslims, and Ibn Saud—the warrior Prince who united the tribes and gave his name to a kingdom. Most of all, it was the desert—the nomad Bedouin whose way of life had changed little over the centuries.

The desert! Here lay the answer, for among the Bedouins we should come close to family life and to traditions that formed the background of modern Saudi Arabia. For months we delved into the possibilities of pursuing this project, and the obvious hazards and barriers to success seemed insurmountable. Would Russ' knowledge of Arabic be enough to gain acceptance by a nomadic people whose customs and laws were strange to us? Could we even find the *bait ash sha'ar*, the hair tent of the Bedouin? Did we have the courage to penetrate the desert with its awesome unknowns?

We resolved to try. Inquiring about the eastern tribes—the Bani Khalid, Ajman, Mutair and Al Murrah—their habits and territories, served to strengthen our interest. We learned they settle on established wells during the suffocating months of summer, and that is no time for amateurs to go exploring. Early fall and spring entice the tribes to distant areas where rains provide water and fodder for camel herds. How far could we go, since half the gasoline we carried must be reserved for getting back?

In early January of 1961, Russ came home with a Land Rover—that marvelous mechanism to which no terrain is impassable, almost. It carried both British and Saudi license plates, and being tan in color, Linda dubbed it the "Jarbu", desert rat. Soon camping gear crowded the corners and rafters of the garage, along with a cache of five gallon cans for extra gasoline and water.

We always signed out at Ras Tanura's Main Gate, stating general direction and expected time of return, in the event search parties became necessary. And we never went without a second car.

During the 1960s, we spent weekends and holidays under the stars on some distant desert known only to God and the Bedu. Sometimes the land was empty save for ourselves. Other times, first rains dotted the plains with black tents. Russ' fluency in the Arabic language opened up the world of the Bedu. The families of the *bait ash sha'ar* warmed to our approach because we were ourselves a family. We never refused their hospitality, though it was sometimes difficult to swallow dried goat cheese tickly with black hairs and gritty with sand. We found the Bedouin interested in us first, as a family and secondly, insofar as we touched his life. It was the women who made our journeys intimate and rewarding.

Muslim tradition prohibits the photographing of women, but being of that sex myself, and sounding the depth of our welcome, gave me courage to use the Hasselblad. Every picture was spontaneously permitted and became a record of a disappearing way of life.

Discovering Arabia of the desert as a reality for our daughters led to other contacts and opportunities. Our departure from the Kingdom in 1971 embraced a farewell to Bedouin friends, to villagers of Jubail, and to the family of His Highness Amir Abdul Mohsin Ibn Jalawi, Governor of the Eastern Province, who taught us all the true meaning of family and home.

How exciting it is to look back on that first excursion of 1961 when all we had was the car, provisions, a compass and the determination to go!

PART 1
The Desert (January 1961)

BEDOUIN CREED
Open land to wander and grass for grazing
A large tent—at least four poles
Wells of sweet water
A beautiful and gentle tempered wife
Many sons and daughters
To live with honor and without shame
To own a sorrel mare, fast as the West Wind
To ride a white *dhulul*
To own great herds of camels and milk camels
Tribesmen of great numbers as followers
To go to Makkah at least once in a lifetime
To have a long life
To be saved from Hell. . . .
To enjoy the rewards of Paradise!

The sun warns the desert of its rising, as a veil of grey light seeps through the night sky like water spilling over a parched land. Soon it will find us, Linda and me, shadowed in the half-light before dawn.

We stand on this limestone ledge, listening to the morning breeze rustling through the sandbed of the *wadi*. It clambers up the escarpment and challenges our invasion of its solitude. Dry stalks from some long lifeless bush crackle, and whirling sand wheels about our legs.

Linda leans against me and shivers. She does not belong to this lonely wilderness of Eastern Arabia that she calls her home. My arm seeks the rounding of her shoulder and pulls her close. Is she afraid of the darkness? Of confrontation with the unknown?

"I'm cold," she whispers.

Her hair, long and loose, flies free of the scarf whose knotted ends flutter about her chin. I finger the topmost button on my daughter's jacket and slip the loop about it.

"It won't be long," I encourage, as the veil of grey light rises.

Behind us, a ragged knoll shelters our nylon tent that strains to follow the wind. The flapping yellow walls fail to arouse my husband, Russ, or daughter, Cyndy, aged seven, still snuggling in sleeping bags. Alongside his red truck, our good friend, Dee Brooks, stirs in a Texan bedroll. Last night Dee had said, "I'll have that coffee chugging on the fire at sunup." And you will, Dee, I think—later, for the sun is not yet here.

On this limestone ledge Linda and I have waited in the darkness and the cold, for she and I made a pact to greet this dawn, to know this land—this ancient culture of the Arabs into which she was born but does not belong.

Through the failing night, a pale orb shimmers in suspension above the *wadi*. Not one, but row on row of awakening moons hang in the darkness. Dawn, touching the concave crescents of the sandhills, has detached them from the blackness of giant shoulders and paused momentarily to reflect her own fragility in the smooth surface of the sand.

The lonely wilderness of eastern Saudi Arabia, as seen from the cave of "Old Crumbly", a *jabal* somewhere beyond As Sarar.

12

The days of yesterday—today
—tomorrow are all sitting on
the dunes, here brocaded with
patterns of rain.

Suddenly, a burst of glory fires the horizon to reveal the hills in their entirety—the red dunes of Arabia—no longer orbs of silver but cauldrons of molten copper.

Day's triumphant birth has arrived many times in Linda's brief life of nine years, but never quite like this birth in the wilderness. It is the day of today—of yesterday—yes, of five thousand years ago. They are all here on the desert—even the day of tomorrow.

Rapidly the splendor of the dunes disappears, lost in the spread of a yellow wash that reveals them for what they are: awesome mountains of sand, grain on endless grain, blowing, reforming, creeping the length of the Arabian Peninsula. The Great Nafud Desert lies to the north. Its sands leap from crested dunes to join the course of the Dahna, a gold-red river of sand, that follows the coastal curves of the Arabian Gulf and on into the Rub' al Khali—the lifeless sweep of the Empty Quarter, most dreaded single wilderness on earth.

Life's freshness is in Linda's face. She is today— tomorrow—not the ancient past, whose moments regroup and mingle with the drifting sand. What do we know of this desert? Russ, a professional technician—or Dee, a Texas lineman—or, I, an American wife? We have been transplanted—the result of Arab nationalism and western enterprise collaborating to release from these wastes the

sources of wealth and economic emergence sealed within rivers of oil. Do we know what it means: the terror of being lost, of a car that breaks down, of water that is gone—of a child's cry unanswered?

Unexpectedly, in this unveiling emptiness, something moves. "It is a man," Linda cries with excitement.

He stands in the flat light, head bowed as though looking for something on the ground. Then he drops to his knees. He is a long way off, but we know what he is doing. Linda has seen it many times in this Muslim land: in the shade of a palm tree as she ran home from school, by the side of the road where she pedalled her bike, in the garden when Ahmad, our house-boy, spread his white *ghutrah* (head scarf) on the coarse grass. The man rises to his feet. He stands very still. In the newness of this day he finds peace; he finds God. In the cold stillness where he stands, he speaks directly to Allah. When the sun is higher and the sands warm, he will speak to Allah again. He will pray four times during the day, and then the last—the fifth—he will kneel again, when the shades of night have closed over everything.

Quietly the man rises, picks up his *ghutrah*, shakes out the sand, and walks off, hidden by the uneven terrain. "Is he a Bedouin?" Linda asks.

Who are they, the Bedouins? Why have they wandered since before the days of Abraham? They are living ancestors whose pride of heritage defies

Bedouin at prayer: In the name of God, Most Gracious, Most Merciful.

Linda and Cyndy share a Bedouin boy's concern for a "Daughter of the Tent". Picture taken in 1964.

the progress of time. On this desert we will find him: this man who has walked these sands for thousands of years. Now he is gone, leaving only the vacant stare of the newborn day.

I follow after Linda, who has aroused the camp with her discovery. Cyndy bounds forward—a chocolate-eyed gamin, soft and melting. Sleep has ruffled her long dark braids, and wisps of hair dance in scattered light across her face. A quick hug, then she scampers after Dee, as he checks the coffee that bubbles on the open fire.

The breeze still lingers in the thin light. Linda spreads her hand toward the flame, and her red boot blocks the escape of a dung beetle burrowing its retreat through the fire's wall.

"I'm hungry!" she calls to Dee.

He sprints toward the truck, and she races after him. The beetle tumbles into spilling sand, and her laughter, like the awakened sky, skims the wastes

Russ and the "*Jarbu*" evaluate
the drop into the wadi.

with cloudless innocence. Breathless, she sags
against the truck's weathered frame, her head
barely reaching the slatted chassis that sits high on
ballooned tires. Dee's truck goes everywhere with
him. Its color is startling red, selected for visibility
through varying degrees of glare and haze. Well
seasoned, rugged, the red truck serves our Land
Rover as mutual protector and backup. A second
set of wheels should our own founder. The rules of
desert driving are adamant: never go out alone,
and never separate from accompanying vehicles.

Friend and companion over many years, Dee
carries in his heart the bright responsiveness of
childhood—the stimulus for life and fun. Deep toned
as an Arab from working shirtless throughout the
scorching summers, he keeps the electrical systems
of the giant oil company operating. I watch him toss
bags of fruit and doughnuts from the rear of the
truck where they are packed in a large wooden
crate bolted to the truck bed.

"How come you don't just lift out the whole
box?" Linda asks.

Dee chuckles. "That box ain't never goin' to
move! I've seen to that!" How well I know the pain
of looking for something stashed in the rear of the
Rover, only to discover it bounced out kilometers
behind!

Breakfast over, Russ and Dee check the engines,
tires, security of extra gas cans, tools and spare auto
parts. Transportation is survival—be it mechanical
wheels or the camel of the Bedu. Leading in the
Land Rover, Russ searches out the smoothest roll
of the ground. He keeps close to the escarpment's
edge, seeking a way into the *wadi*. Are we the first
to come here, to meet what has always been: the
lava rocks, the dried brush, the chains of dunes, the
continuation that never ends? And the silence.
The sun alone speaks in tones of glare and shadow,
of lightness and darkness.

"I'm going to try for that saddle," Russ explains,
pointing toward a distant roll of ground against a
projecting ledge.

From the moment he arrived in Arabia, Russ set
out to learn the language and the customs of this
land. He sought the Saudi Arab in offices, villages
and oases—from *amir* to our own houseboy. They
liked him, trusted him, welcomed him. He senses
many things. You can see it in his eyes as he drives,
evaluating the challenge of changing slopes,
merging drifts, deceit of distance, the dunes sliced

sheer on the opposite side, the crusted flat
treacherously bogged below the surface. Tricks
of the *jinn*, the Bedu say, to bedevil and confuse.

The saddle and a rutted watercourse prove
traversable for the cars. Soon the escarpment slips
behind us, and we roll onto the lower level and the
wadi. Space absorbs the course we followed, now
shapeless and unrecognizable.

"Truck coming?" Russ asks Linda. She sits alone
in the back seat, for Cyndy rides with Dee.

The truck lags behind our dustcloud, and Russ
pursues his course. I try to point out the terrain
where we saw the man, but cannot relate the
remembered topography of sunrise to the fusing
contours as we drive. The desert has changed. Its
components are the same—yet, not, as the pieces
of a kaleidoscope never revolve back to a familiar
shape.

The car slows and loses traction in the sand.
Russ shifts down. The wheels spin, then begin to
roll. It is a laboring swerving and sliding, gaining
and losing. He forces the car toward a clump of
sand-packed brush. The wheels strike with a jolt,
and the tires grip with a suddenness that propels
us forward. Soon the main body of the *wadi* spreads
ahead, rolling pebbled ground with scattered *arfaj*
bushes, and the sandhills recede behind.

"Dee coming?" Russ calls again.

Linda leans forward. "What, Dad?"

"Dee—can you see him?"

The chassis of the Land Rover rattles and bangs
louder than the roar of the engine, or the whistle of
air under the double roof and through every crack
and seam. Linda peers through the dust-covered
window. How dependent we are on visual aid!
Why, we couldn't hear Cyndy shout, nor Dee yell,
nor the horn blare! Don't lose sight of that truck!

"There he is!" Linda says. "But—not exactly
following."

The ground is firm and the going good. On either
side, ridged drifts close in to meet us. Dunes, once
rose red, wander rusty in a yellow wash, so evenly
applied no thickened drip relieves the monotony.

Linda leans close to her father's shoulder. "Dad,
I think I lost Dee. I can't see the truck."

The motor's pitch shifts audibly. "He made the
wadi. He's got to be behind," Russ declares.

"But, he's not, Dad." The car jams to a stop.
Linda says, "There was dust over there—but it's
gone."

17

Light and shadow alter the
inconstant face of the land.

A rising well of fear. Russ springs from the car.
He stares through our settling dust cloud, tracing
the route we traveled. The land is empty. Once
Linda shouts, "There he is!" But it is only the spiral
of a *jinn*—a desert whirlwind—blowing itself away.
All eyes probe empty space, seeking the red truck.
Cyndy and Dee. They could be but a few yards away,
yet lost by a thousand kilometers of uncertainty.
A merciless giant, taunting, chuckling at the
anguish of amateurs who come to challenge, has
swallowed up the tiny splotch of red.

We drive to a low rise, then get out to search the
desert again. Seconds become eternities under the
beating sun and the never changing view. Where in
this vastness sits the moment that held a child's
embrace—tender and warm? Russ touches my
shoulder. "Look," he directs.

In the distance, the desert floor rolls, undulates
with moving mounds, pulsing visibly one after the
other, as if a mass migration of sand. Only it is not
sand. It is camels! Shuffling, pacing, rocking, the
beasts spread over the land in an even, rolling
motion. Space in rhythm, rocking in and out of the
centuries. And—oh joy!—on the fringe of the herd
an unmistakable show of red. Instantly we are in
the car. We dive over rocks, ruts and jutting
limestone. Thank goodness for the Rover's low, low
gear—that yellow knob on the floor next to the gear
shift that locks down to keep us from plunging faster.

Dee and Cyndy wave as we come up. They were
not lost! They had waited for the camels. And we
didn't know where they were, for the desert hangs
onto its secrets. I stand by the Rover still shaken
from fear and the desperation of that final plunge.

Seeking a direction across the trackless desert of Saudi Arabia's Eastern Province.

A shuffling camel herd rocks in and out of the centuries.

Curly coated babies stop and bawl. They are all stick legs and enormous eyes.

The engine's heat swirls under the raised hood, and dust settles thick and clinging on the car, as though the flying components of the desert would bury it. But I am whole again, for a slim arm wraps snugly about my waist.

"We saw them first!" Cyndy cries.

"Next time you tell Dee to stick with us," I admonish.

"We couldn't. The truck wouldn't go."

In the full brilliance of the sun I am chilled. Had I the right to bring them, these daughters who belong to the future? Strangely, something outside myself has made me stronger than fear. It issues from those many hearts beating in compact concentration, as the succession of beasts moves on. A feeling of peace infiltrates my consciousness. I live again dawn's awakening of the dunes. Beyond the herd's shuffling feet, a lone man still kneels and prays:

"Allah, the Merciful, the Compassionate."

Cyndy watches Dee and Russ delve into the engine of the truck. Its motion is stalled, and we can no longer continue. Linda calls me to join her, as she hurries closer to the herd. We listen to the hiss of air freed from the sand by forward marching hooves. It gathers into voice, undertones of man's need across the ages, songs of rejoicing that found birth in this wilderness.

"The Lord is my shepherd. I shall not want."

Words of life. So short a time ago life existed only in ourselves. Now it abounds. They are only beasts, but they will take life when they go.

We distinguish the ragged wool dangling in tufts from their backs, the calloused knees long couched, eyes thick lashed and fluid. Curly coated babies stumble and cry. They are all stick legs, heads and enormous eyes. Their double-jointed limbs fling in all directions. They stop, and huddle, and bawl. The pungent odor stifles. A head on a long neck swings in our direction. Its cavernous mouth slits wide and spits with a rumbling regurgitation.

We pause for breath. A shrill whistle shrieks. "Dad!" Linda cries, responding to a familiar signal.

The truck and the Rover summon from the rise. The camels move on, absorbing moments we shared into the continuance of their caravans. We start back toward the cars, but are stopped by a camel rider who lopes directly toward us.

He rides at a low, lop-sided gait, colored tassels swinging from the saddle and cloak billowing

20

The white camel halts, and from its great height the *sheikh* gazes down on us.

The Ajman *sheikh* and tribesman continue their search for new grasses.

behind. The white camel halts, and from its great height the man gazes down on us. He lays his camel stick across the leg hooked over the tall pommel and leans his arms on it. Linda steps forward, but I pull her back. How easily this lord of the desert could swing down and carry her off!

I find words. "*As salaam alaikum*—God's peace upon you." These words of greeting are not of my language, and this man is not of my understanding. I stand fearful before him.

The Bedouin holds me with his gaze, piercing, direct. Then a smile breaks the fierceness of his countenance, and his response gives us the peace of Allah.

The man does not couch his beast, as the cars approach, but swings the animal about, as if comparing our Land Rover with his handsome mount. She is young—a *dhulul* (female riding camel)—slender and finely boned with lips carved into a perpetual smile. How regal the rider appears sitting high above us, his cloak hanging comfortably on his shoulders. The cloth is of light brown wool trimmed in gold braid, and a red and white checked *ghutrah* drapes to shade his eyes. He sits on a curly, black sheepskin that covers the saddle of pomegranate wood. Underneath, the hollow about the hump is padded with a sack of straw, a roll of bedding and a handsome colored rug. Bulging saddlebags hang from either side. They are of white homespun, embroidered in red and black and ornamented with tassels.

Cyndy runs from the cars to get to us, but she is stopped, as the camel swings toward her. The Bedouin reaches down, arm extended to touch the child.

"*Fiamanillah*, (Go, God with you)," he calls, circling his mount around us. He taps his stick against the neck of the *dhulul*. With a quick upward flick of her tail and stiffening of joints, the camel springs into a trot.

"*Fiamanilkarim*," Russ calls after him. "Where are you going?"

"Only Allah knows." Soon the camel is one with
the sand.

"Why didn't you stop Cyndy from getting too
close?" I demand of Russ. "That man could
have . . ."

"She was in no danger."

"How do you know?" I say, annoyed by his
assurance.

"He is a *sheikh* (tribal leader) of the Ajman," Russ
explains, ". . . the tribe that roams this *dirrah*
(territory). We are in his tribal territories."

Cyndy interrupts. "Look what he gave me."
A polished stone lies on her open palm.

"Hey—let's see that," Dee breaks in. He rolls the
orange oval between his fingers. "Looks like one of
those rocks my crew boys find in the Rub' al Khali."

"Can't be, Dee," I say. "This one is so highly
polished."

"That's right," Dee agrees. "By the desert."

The desert. How quickly is judgment passed on
the unknown. Within time's infinity all is possible:
the survival of the human spirit above total
desolation; the beauty of a polished stone, known
but to the wind and the ages. From horizon to
horizon the eyes see only dry and barren ground.
We cannot follow this Bedouin and his camel. We
are limited by our own mechanical capacities.
When half our gasoline is gone, we must turn back.

"Why didn't you call Cyndy?" I ask Russ, as we
start toward the cars.

"She was in no danger. The man came by the
cars to ask if we needed help. I said I was waiting for
you, and he rode off to find you. A man who offers
his hand as a brother is not a man to be feared."

Dee points off into the distance. "Hey, Russ, how
about headin' for that pinnacle yonder?" The two
men set the floating compass on the ground, away
from the cars' magnetic field, and sight the direction.

"Due east plus a degree, I read," Russ says.

"Yup—I'll take ya up on that," Dee agrees,
squinting into the dial.

"Can't you just see it and go there?" Linda asks.

"My land, ya'd better not try!" Dee answers.
"Why, by the time you go six yards, that rock'll look
like something you never saw before."

Even if we miss the pinnacle, at least due east
will take us eventually to the Arabian Gulf, the
Trans-Arabian pipeline and home. We do not reach
it. The way is bogged, and the cars keep to higher
ground. We go back to the dunes, to a low chain,
and angle up the crusty slopes. It is long and tedious
and tiring, and the day seems never to end. The sun
is always high, the glare always blinding, the way
never finding a conclusion—as a city street reaches
an intersection or a dead end. And so we just go
on, until we stop at the top of a pebbled rise.

"Hey—look! Tents!" Linda cries.

We get out and stare, stunned at facing the
absolute.

"I can count eight," Cyndy says.

But I can count more. The handful of black
shapes stretched across the ground relate the
infinite folding, and moving, and building of
goathair tents since first the nomad wandered.

PART II
The Mudhole (January 1961)

IN THE DESERT THE GROUP RULES
Oh, girl with the red dress
Many a man would like that
You become his bride,
But the one who failed
To join the group cannot
Be your man.
He who is away for a good cause
Ought not to be blamed.

The whole of the world's past fills the emptiness. It crowds the sky, the desolate flat, the sandhills beyond. Not as a date to be filed for future reference, but as existence—a day that always is. I stand on this pebbled knoll, facing the impact of truth. Those long roofs of black—*bait ash sha'ar*, the hair tent of the Bedouin—have crossed the centuries, as they have crossed the wastes. Now, their time is ours . . .

Within a circle of bare hills, we look down upon a natural basin scooped out as from some huge sandpile. The nakedness is terrible. No dry brush nor withered grass—just endless, sterile ground, rising up and over the hills who knows how far. Pegged to the nothingness stand two rows of perhaps a dozen long, black tents—broad strokes of a thick lead pencil on a blank page, as though Linda had scrawled them on her first day of kindergarten. They appear to be devoid of life.

I peer through the pigmented haze in search of something that links us, the twentieth century, with this moment of the ancient past. A tangible fusion of extremities, as the sea flows momentarily upon the shore and, retreating, leaves its mark on the sand. This common presence of ages, thousands of years separated, must carry one thread of unity.

Through the yellow glare of the sun a child appears—as Cyndy is a child—clinging to the weathered wall of its home. And I have found it—that common ground: human life.

A hundred meters from the first tent, a group of camels huddles together. The beasts are motionless, as if cut and pasted from scraps of cardboard. Some stand, long necks outstretched. Others couch on the ground. Two are in motion, as a rider directs them away from the camp.

"What d'ya say we catch them!" Dee challenges. He leaps into the truck, the girls after him.

The truck roars in an arc down the knoll, and Russ and I follow in the Rover. I feel no compulsion to go after the camels, only a need to collect myself in my time, and then to walk into the past. The cars dodge the wind-ripped gashes along the rocky edge of the basin, as with searching fingers the blowing ground sand settles into the unevenness. Already the tents are gone, enfolded by the slopes. Ahead,

Through the sun's glare I distinguish a child, clinging to the weathered wall of its home.

Pegged to the nothingness
stand two rows of long, black
tents—the *bait ash sha'ar* of
the Bedouin.

the beasts tread rhythmically, gracefully in a continuous motion. Our vehicles bounce and swerve, their rigid joints and seams unyielding to the terrain.

A *sabkhah* (salt flat) stretches ahead. Its top is curled in giant flakes baked crisp by the sun. Camels have trod a path over the swampy salt flat, but the cars cannot cross the swirling, unsettled bog of sand, salt and water below that crackled surface.

Dee jumps from the truck, cups his hands about his mouth and shouts. The Bedouin shifts in the saddle, adjusts his white *ghutrah* across his face, but does not stop. The camels pace on, their flexible footpads spread and mold to the ground they tread. A prod with the camel stick erupts the rider's mount into a jog. Rumbling complaints roll from the beast's belly, as water slops and streams from the huge black container roped to each side of the saddle.

We join Dee by the *sabkhah*.

"That's an innertube!" Linda exclaims, pointing to the container the camel carries.

"Sure isn't a dried camelskin," Dee teases. A dried camelskin is the usual container for long hauls of water.

"How far will he take it—all that water?" Cyndy asks.

"Twenty kilometers, maybe," her father replies. "To a camp without a well."

It is not the rising sun I watch, but it is an enlightenment. The Bedouin and his solitary march arouse an awareness of his fortitude: his skill in locating a specific spot on this desert—faith in his ability to survive— to face uncertainty day after day: a dry waterhole, a camel gone lame, hunger.

Could we do that? Give ourselves to suffering and to hostility? Or, go as he goes, giving himself to

28

The camel rider brings water
to a distant encampment
without a well.

Could we go as he goes—
giving himself to God, he and
his women and his children?

God—he and his women and his children . . .

The Rover's motor catches fuel and roars.
"Coming, El?" Russ calls. He leans from the car.
"We're going back to the tents."

The sun makes a mirror of his dark glasses and
excites the bold plaid of his shirt. In him is me, yet I
cannot follow. Truth's credibility wavers. I must
reach the face of the *bait ash sha'ar* on foot, as any
stranger from the desert. I approach the side where
he sits at the wheel.

"Look—you go on. I'm going to walk."

"Walk!"

"Back to the tents. I can see one from here." At
the base of a long ridge of hillocks, a single black
line writes its identity on the monotonous yellow
ground.

"That's ridiculous! Get in."

My mind is made up. "It's not far. Linda can
come with me, and we'll meet you back at the
encampment."

The Rover swings about, then follows the lead of
the truck. A whirling dust screen rises behind the
cars. I watch until it dissipates. We are alone, Linda
and I, with only scattered pebbles along the tire
tracings to tell how we got here. A gust of air rushes
across the basin, billowing Linda's yellow blouse.
I shiver—but not with the chill of the wind. It is the
hostile desert laughing—the unfinished past—the
sense of my own inadequacy that make me aware:
"I want to live!"

We start walking. My gaze holds the distant tent.
That thin, black line must not mirage in a vaporous
dance, like the yellow lizard scurrying beyond
Linda's reach among the blackened stones of a
deserted campfire. To walk. To put one foot in front
of the other and tread the path of history toward a
tent and the crush of camels about a well. To
exchange security for hazard, comfort for suffering.
Civilization for freedom, anxiety for peace. How
shattering to mind and body, this expulsion without
transition.

One tent stands apart from the rest. Its heavy
worsted roof dips between the poles that are set
three across the face—the front. The color is not
wholly the black of goathair, but laced with deep
brown, a natural hue found in the black wool of the
desert sheep. The cloth is thick, tightly woven, and
weighs on the poles.

Frayed and bleached with large knots and
dangling ends to show where the strain has snapped

them, the long support ropes reach out for distant
pegs and hold the hair roof taut. The ground
adjacent is strewn with piles of refuse: bits of rags
and threads of rope, tufts of animal hair, scraps of
dried leather. The animal droppings, so like the dung
beetle that bears their name, give a pebbled texture
to the ground. The dung is more profuse closer to
the tent. Soon these families must move on. Perhaps
even tomorrow the poles will be pulled and tied, the
collapsed tent rolled toward the middle, the
furnishings collected, and all roped to the backs of
camels. This camp where we stand will be empty,
left to the wind and sun to sweep and sanitize the
refuse of human habitation and the defecation of
animals. Now there is no one here—no indication
of human life.

The face of the tent is closed in by a strip of
worsted hooked to the roof. It is woven in black and
white stripes, a favorite design of the Ajman tribe.
A white curtain, embroidered in black and red,
divides the tent into two rooms. On one side of the
qata (the dividing curtain) is the *mahram*, the
women's quarters. On the other, the *majlis*, the area
reserved for men and guests. I stand back, not
wishing to peer over that closed wall.

Nearby, a long strip of newly woven roofing
stretches between pegs. A large container, partly
filled with dirty water, stands alongside. Someone
has been soaking the cloth and left it to weather in
the sun. Linda fidgets uneasily.

"Let's find Dad," she says.

"There's nothing to be afraid of," I say.

Her eyes flash. "That's not what Mehedi said . . ."

The aged Saudi carpenter who came to my house
to make a pair of picture frames had told us that
Bedouins were unfriendly. "Mehedi is a villager,"
I tell her, "and they don't like the Bedu." My words
carry little assurance. I have even less
understanding than Mehedi. And unreality
persists: the emptiness, the absence of human
sounds, the awareness of trespassing.

"Let's go." Linda says. "They don't want us
here."

We start to turn away but are held by the clatter
of a can that crashes to the ground behind us. I hear
a muffled scream and the slosh of water. A black
robed figure rushes past, sand flying from bare feet.
I catch a glimpse of the unmasked face of a young
girl, eyes glistening with fear. One hand clutches her
robe at the chin, and water drips from the heavy

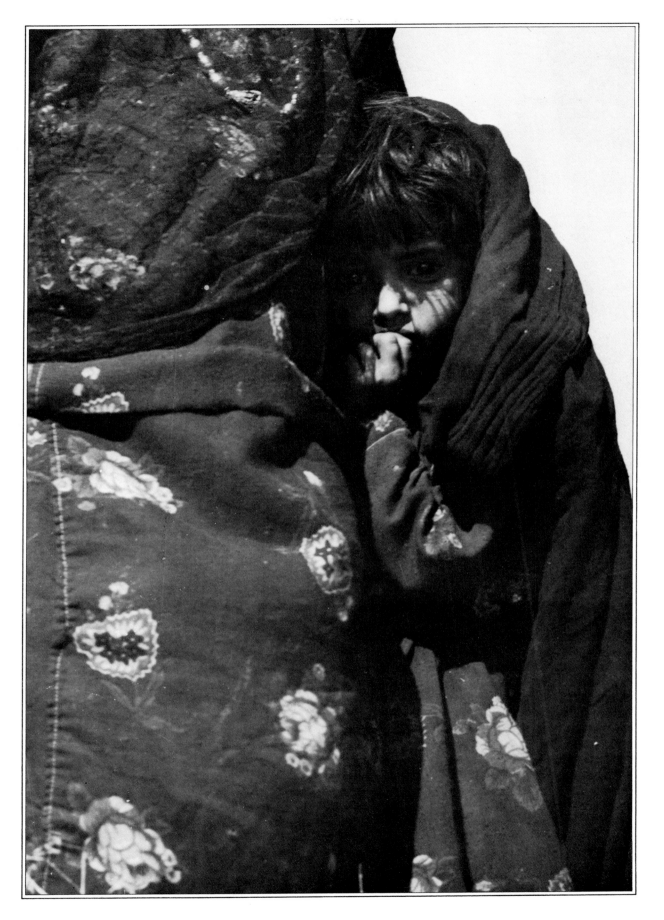

Top: The home of an Ajman family located in the vicinity of As Sudayrah. The face, or front, is closed in against the wind.

Bottom: A newly woven strip of roofing weathers in the sun.

The Bedouin girl stares at Linda as if to ask: ''Who is this stranger? Where did she come from?''

Animals repose about a pool
of scum covered water—a
mudhole that is life to men
and animals alike.

The boy toys with his *ghutrah*,
staring at us with uncertainty.

skirt. She stumbles in her rush to reach the tent,
free hand clawing at the closed curtains.

"What happened!" Linda gasps.

"I'm not sure," I say, turning and seeing no one
else. "I guess we frightened her." The girl's cry has
unnerved me. I am reluctant to look back toward
the tent, but stare at the spilled water, as it is sucked
into the ground.

Voices argue within the tent. The curtain bulges
and parts, as a pair of red-sleeved arms pushes the
girl outside. Immediately, she dives to crawl under
the tent, but a woman emerges, grabs the girl about
the waist and swings her into the open. For a
moment, the girl stands alone, facing us. Panicked,
she rushes the tent. There is a brief scuffle, then a
fluttered giggle behind the woman's mask. It is a
game to determine who will approach the strangers.
With a push, the woman propels the girl toward us.

"*Ta'aaliy . . .*" I say. "Come here."

Slowly, the girl's hand withdraws from her face.
The dark eyes focus beyond me, on Linda. Bedouin
fortitude brings her close and without fear. Her
hand reaches out, as if to touch the fair stranger:

the pale skin tones, the loose hair, the high red
boots, the bright yellow blouse. Her feet are
calloused, her hands hennaed, the cloth of her long
black robe stained and grimy. Tufts of unkempt hair
cast shadows across her face. The touch of her
rough skinned fingers is gentle. But all else fades
beneath the profound searching of her eyes: deep
pools of concentration and wonderment probing
the meaning of this stranger she could not possibly
understand existed.

And then she smiles. For one brief moment a
human relationship makes us one.

Then the moment is no more.

"*Imsh!*"

A man strides across the open ground, green
thaub (long robe) slapping his legs. He orders the
woman and girl into the tent, then faces me in
anger. "*Imsh!*" he shouts again, shaking a fist.
"Leave! This is my country! My people! My home!
I do not want you here! *Imsh!*"

And we go, but, what had we done wrong? The
curtains of the centuries are not as easily unrolled
as the embroidered *qata* of a black tent. Ahead,

Ali al Ajmi and his tribal family cling to the peace and freedom of the desert.

women and children flurry in and out of the double line of tents.

"I want to find Dad," Linda says, as she turns away. I, too, feel the need for his nearness.

A string of camels threads down the distant sandhills, the leader heading for the encampment, but there is no sign of the cars. I shield my eyes from stray sand, as a vagrant wind whirls across the basin. It comes from the northwest, forerunner of the violent *shamal* of spring. Linda's cheeks are pink, her eyes bright, and she swings her arms as she walks.

The assemblage of couched camels is within range. The ground about them is dank and defiled. We hesitate before entering into the oppressive odor of beasts, but hopefully, the cars are on the other side. The animals' backs are to the wind. Long necks criss-cross as we pass. The revolting vocalizing from their solid bulk is enough to frighten any stranger. We reach a clearing where a woman stands as though challenging the bare land, the nagging wind fluttering the tatters of her dress. She empties a leather bucket of water into a huge, black tub. The veil is blown from her face, and her hair is caught in loose, uncombed braids.

She smiles at us and beckons. Then, back erect, she squats, raises the tub to her head and stands, balancing the tub with both hands. Stiffly, she pivots on bare feet to face us. "*Yalla! Yalla!*" she calls. "Come!" Her lips quiver in a shrill trill, as she nudges aside the herd and heads for the open ground and tents beyond. But we do not follow.

Ahead spreads a patch of stale and sodden ground, blackened by perpetual use and stagnant with the quiet stench of centuries. Animals and various receptacles repose about a pool of scum covered water. Here is nothing more than a mudhole to be violated by the excrement of animals, to be dried up in summer, and to be blown over by the driving sands of countless *shamal* (sand storm). The mudhole, brackish and filthy, is life to men and animals alike.

Her smile beckoned us to share her home—even the water, but I cannot relate to what I see, nor appreciate the thankfulness of a traveler who has lost his way and comes upon this pool. Linda's comprehension is less than mine. Her concern is not with the mudhole, but with something else beyond. Across the pool, a young boy in a blue striped *thaub* waits patiently while his horse drinks from a rusty

tub. He appears uneasy, staring at us with the same startled look as the girl's. He leans against the horse's neck for the same security we need, and stands one foot on top of the other in a timeless gesture of childhood embarrassment. It is the horse that excites Linda—a desert mare all bundled up in rags! She calls to the boy, as though he lived next door.

"Is she yours?"

The boy frowns. Her language is strange. We are strange! His skin is cracked and dry, his *thaub* torn, but the way he leans his head against the horse is a gesture of love. Linda steps closer to the mudhole and gasps at the mare's unpared hooves, the matted tail, the scars of burns on her legs. How different she is from my daughters' own Arab mares, stabled, well groomed and carefully fed.

"What's her name?" Linda's voice is eager.

The boy toys with the tip of his white *ghutrah*, running it across his lip. As long as we look at him, he remains motionless like a wild and trapped creature.

The camels come to life. They nudge and grumble, disturbed from lethargy. I duck, as a hideous head swings close, green saliva frothing from its jaws. I step with caution through the muck about the pool, away from the camels—antiquated, bad-tempered as the land. Some of the animals move away, as a man prods through them and walks toward me. Where is Russ? Where the cars? If this man chases us off, what shall we do? I call Linda to come back, but she does not. She stands fascinated on the edge of the black pool.

The boy drags a leather bucket from the water, disturbing the scum. The snaking rope dislodges scattered dung. Several pieces roll along the ground into the waterhole. Linda jumps forward to stop them with her boot.

The man's laugh is good-natured. "Allah's bounty is for the animals, as well as for his people." This is not the voice of one who would turn us away. He stands beside me—tall and handsome, despite the ravages of smallpox that scar his face. "To know the camel is to appreciate its worth. We Bedu could not survive without them."

"I'm sorry," I say. "They are frightening." It comes to me that these are sounds I know, for the newcomer is speaking English. And, best of all, behind him follow Russ, Dee and Cyndy—barely visible above a running blockade of small boys who

tug and chatter around them. The ages slip away. No longer must I grope to find a niche for myself in this past.

"That is my son." The man's tones are quiet, friendly, proud. "Hassan Ibn Ali al Ajmi. Yes—I speak your language a little, but nothing like your husband knows ours."

"You do me too much honor, Ali," Russ says. "It is I who lack the true understanding of your language and your people."

"But you care," Ali replies. "That is important."

As Ali speaks, Hassan pulls on the rope about the mare's muzzle, swings the animal around, leaps to its back and races toward the tents.

"How fast she is! And how her tail flags!" Linda cries. "Can we ride her?" She starts to run.

"Hold on there, knothead," Dee calls, going after her.

As Ali leads the way to the tents, he explains that some years ago he worked for the oil company. He learned to speak English and to drive a truck. He earned more *riyal* than he had ever seen in his whole life. He didn't like exchanging loose clothing for the confining trousers of the westerner, his sandals for high-toed safety shoes, the night sky for a bed in a dormitory. He saved his money and returned to his clan with prestige and honor. Now leader of his people, he will never again relinquish the freedom and dignity of the Bedouin.

Outside the circle of animals, a man and a boy stand on either side of a small donkey. The boy watches us as we pass. He is barefooted, his frayed and buttonless jacket little comfort against the biting wind. His companion wears only a thin summer garment. Without taking his gaze from us, the boy continues stuffing a sack from a large pile of dried camel droppings. Cyndy stops to stare, eyes wide and questioning. I explain that they are collecting desert fuel, but she frowns.

"What would you use, if you had no firewood?"

Her hesitation conveys reluctant understanding. "I don't know. But I'd think of something!" she says.

Ali is amused. "In my tent we shall have coffee. You will see what a good fire I can make."

From under the fringed overhang of the nearest tent, an animal slinks out, craftily hugging itself to the ground. An ominous growl vibrates in a taut throat, as the animal works its way behind us. Ali shouts a command, and the dog returns unwillingly to its hole under the flap.

Linda and Dee stand looking at the mare, now tethered in front of Ali's tent.

"So you like my Murrawiyyah," Ali says. "The Prophet has said: 'The expression in a horse's eye is like a blessing on a good man's house.'"

About two years old, the mare has a shaggy ginger colored coat with black mane and tail. For protection against the cold, she wears an odd assortment of wrappings that hang to her knees: bits of torn tent strips, old saddlebags, grain sacks and pieces of an *aba* (winter cloak). What a rag-bag she looks in her patches and tassels, all tied around her belly with a length of rope! The mare's foreleg wears an iron shackle that is chained to a post driven into the ground. Linda protests that they ought to use a rope.

"A rope," Ali answers. "Good for the mare, yes. But too good for the one who would steal her from me."

That was in the old days—merely thirty years ago from this day of 1961. Tribes raided each other's encampments in *ghazu*. What you didn't have you took. "Murrawiyyah is fast," Ali continues. "And justly named 'The Wind'. And she is gentle—very gentle—a true daughter of my tent." Proudly, he lauds her bloodlines. No written pedigree. All remembered . . .

Cyndy listens, entranced. Her dark eyes glow, as she turns to Ali. "Could I ride her? Could I?"

Hassan scowls. The mare is ridden only by the master and the son. I do not want Cyndy to ride. We know nothing of this desert pony. I divert her attention toward two black clothed figures hastening along the drafty corridor of tents: a woman and a girl bearing high bundles of *arfaj* on their heads. Children converge on them in warning. The girl runs off, her gathered sticks falling to the ground behind her. The woman moves slowly toward us, stops, throws her bundle down, and rushes inside a tent. The imprint of her body billows the coarse cloth wall, as she peers through a slit below the roof. After a moment, she reappears then slips into another tent closer to us.

I nudge Russ. "I'm taking the girls to the next tent. Okay?"

He turns from Ali. "Don't be long. We're invited for coffee."

Coffee! The obscenity of the mudhole has suddenly become mine. "Oh, no, Russ—we just can't!" His silence is disapproval enough. His eyes

Murrawiyyah, Ali's mare, all
bundled up in her patches and
tassels.

Following page : The vicinity of
As Sudayrah where Ali came
to look for salt bush for his
camels.

A Bedouin mother, her *abayah*
salt stained and ballooned by
the wind, seeks help for her
ill child.

carry a message: be as they are—do as they do. But,
I cannot—then, an inspiration. "Bargain for the
mare! That will take all day, and there'll be no time
for coffee."

I call Cyndy, but she won't come. Russ puts his
arm around her and turns his back on the tent
families. The woman comes out and beckons boldly,
as Linda and I walk to meet her.

Unexpectedly, the woman is upon me, her
ballooning *abayah* (woman's black cloak) a signal
of distress. The anxiety in her eyes is intensified by
the cloth covering her face. Words tangle with
excited gestures, as she grabs my arm and leads me
to the tent. She parts the curtains and waits. I
beckon Linda to follow, then duck beneath the
heavy roof, and step into the veiled interior.

Escape from the sun's glare momentarily blocks
my vision, then, through the dimness, shadows
take shape: the personal belongings of a nomad
family. On the ground lie sacks of supplies, a straw
mat, metal pots and bowls. The high hoops of the
maksar (woman's camel litter) dominate the center
of the room, and at the rear goatskins hang from a
rough tripod. Nomadic life has taken its toll on
everything—and everyone—exposed as they are to
the extremes of heat and cold, the sandpaper action
of *shamal*, the lashing and rocking on the backs
of camels.

A high-pitched, scaleless wail directs my gaze
toward the woman, who hovers above a child lying
on a red quilt. The girl is listless, and her eyes reveal
that liquid look of fever. No interpreter need
translate a mother's plea for her child. The polluted
mudhole, the icy winds, tents never really drying
out during the rainy season, the animal droppings
dotting the floor, the close proximity of many people
sleeping together within the small space of the tent:
all are conducive to illness. Gradually the tent fills
with women and girls, lining themselves silently
along the wall, or squatting on the ground. All dark
shapes waiting, staring at me.

From the pocket of my jacket I remove a tin of
aspirin. "*Miyah* . . ." I say, calling for water. The
mother's wail rises. She gathers the child into her
arms and, rocking tenderly, leans her masked face
against the damp cheek. "*Miyah*," I repeat, pointing
to the goatskins.

One of the silent figures picks up a metal bowl
from the floor, shaking off a chicken that perched on
the rim. She unlashes the neck of the goatskin, and

water flows through the long, dark hairs. I daren't
look at what else might lie inside that bowl. I place
two aspirin in the mother's hand.

"For the child—*bintik*—with water."

A brief respite from fever. Is this all my advanced
world can offer an obsolete existence? Again I
search my pocket. Into the small, warm hand I
place a roll of candy—bright of color, sweet of
taste . . .

I leave the tent chastened by the realization of my
own inadequacy to overcome what the desert has
decreed.

"We've been bargaining for the horse!" Cyndy
rushes us, as Linda and I return.

"You mean, we can buy her?" Linda's excitement
is contagious.

"How'll we ever get her home!" I exclaim.

"She's not ours—exactly," Cyndy says. "Tell
them, Dad."

But it is Ali who explains that each of four cousins
in remote parts of the *dirrah* owns a share in the
belly of the horse. Perhaps in five years when the
debts have been paid in foals, we might have a
chance to buy the fifth one. The mare is never sold.
Then Ali turns to Cyndy. "Let your daughter
ride . . ."

Hassan unshackles the mare and boosts Cyndy
to Murrawiyyah's back. Instantly, the mare is in
motion.

Dee shouts: "Don't let her have her head!" But
the horse wears neither rein nor bit, merely a
risan—a single rope of colored wool.

We all watch, as the swift Murrawiyyah races
down the line of tents, Cyndy squeezing her knees
against the flapping rags. Ali tells us he is of the
Ajman tribe—*sharif*, noble—an ancestral status
reflected in his face, not his raiment. His clan
traverses the tribal territories in the lower sands and
gravel plains of Al Hasa in the Eastern Province.
He has come into As Sudayrah to look for salt bush
for his camels, an area marked by the mudhole and
a nearby crumbling fort. Guide, tracker, decision
maker, counselor, judge, father, protector, story
teller, enforcer of the faith—Ali is all these to his
tribal family. As he talks, he braids long strands of
horsehair into a rope.

Cyndy turns the mare at the farthest tent and
races her back. But we are not the only ones who
watch. An old woman slips out of Ali's tent and

The liquid look of fever mists the child's eyes.

The child in her elaborate but faded dress reminds me of Joseph and his coat of many colors.

squats on the ground several paces ahead of us. She wraps her cloak closely about her head.

Cyndy returns in triumph. I hurry to meet her, along with a rush of small boys and girls. But the old woman gets there first. Hands outstretched, she clasps the quivering muzzle, black head bowed above the pulsing nostrils, and kisses the soft, pink flesh above the mare's lips. And I know the gentle disposition of the desert mare is the result of such love showered on it by the women and children of the black tents.

"*Alhamdulillah!*" she cries, praising Allah for my daughter's return. Honoring the rider as she has the mare, she clasps Cyndy's boot in both hands and bends low to kiss the toe—a delicate tracery of veil patterning the dust.

Beside me, Ali protests with a smile. "My mother."

Beyond the site of Murrawiyyah's return, a tiny child dances among the tent ropes that intertwine in a lacing of common dependency. Her dress is colorful, though faded, and she pauses now and then as a startled gazelle before taking off in flight.

It calls to me—this wisp of color in all the

drabness, and I must return to the tents. My presence disturbs her play, and the child stops fluttering about.

"*Ta'aaliy,*" I call, kindly. "Come here." But she will not stay. I call her again; she scampers under a curtain.

Linda catches up with me. "Dad's getting ready to leave," she says.

But I must find that child. We walk the line of tents, aware of bodies pressing against the walls from the inside. How many eyes peer through the peepholes in the homespun for a glimpse of strangers from another time? I call again, and the sounds of giggling betray those who listen behind the walls.

"Mom, it's their house. They don't want us." Linda pulls me away.

Behind us the curtains part, and a voice calls out, "*Ba'ad daqiqah*—wait."

A woman stands in front of the tent holding the tiny child by the hand. She nods with a half smile, picks up the little girl, and nestles her tenderly in her arms. She brushes sand from the soft cheeks and straightens the medallion of beads dangling on the forehead from the hood. Then she covers her own face with a veil.

I raise the camera, focusing on the colorful robe, the brilliant beads, the wide eyes—evoking the image of someone else who had a robe of many colors, a child who lived in a black tent. Joseph, the favorite of his father—here today, as he was yesterday, and will be tomorrow.

Linda waits near Ali's tent. Russ and the others have crossed a wide slope of ground that separates the encampment from the cars. I hurry to catch up, but a woman blocks the way—the mother of the sick child. She pushes a circlet of yellow bells into my hand. Attached to one end is a bead of turquoise, appeaser of evil spirits. A gift for a gift. A bracelet for an aspirin—token of affinity between us.

Linda and I step into the open area beyond Ali's tent. A warning growl rips the air, as a bristling brown body springs into action and bars the way. Tent dogs! Hunched down, fangs bared and backs bristling, three watchdogs have us cornered. Ugly in their ferocity and half starved to increase their meanness, our every step provokes them to lunge.

Thank goodness for Linda's high boots! Though these beasts could grip a throat as easily as an ankle.

Someone must call them off. Over there—a disappearing green *thaub*. I shout. There is no response. I grab the strap of the heavy cameracase and swing it toward the nearest dog. It slinks back. I catch Linda's hand and together we start to run. Long trained to flush out intruders and wolves, the animals soon have us encircled.

We wait for the attack. Instead, a girl's voice calls out. She stands in the fold of a tent, a tuft of hair shadowing her face. Her tones are sharp and commanding. With a dying snarl, the dogs slink off to hide in their holes at the edge of the roof.

We reach the cars. Russ is already in the Rover, and Dee is warming up the truck's motor. Cyndy

calls from the cabin, as she holds out a length of braided horsehair rope.

"Hey, look! Ali made it for me from Murrawiyyah's tail—a promise I can have one of her foals."

Ali watches as the cars churn the dust. "*Fiamanillah*," he calls. Go, God with you. There is no other way.

I turn for a last look at the encampment. Women collect in groups. Children dart about. The girl who touched us with understanding still stands by the tent. I wave my thanks, and she runs off toward the farthest *bait ash sha'ar*, where once again a fleeting glimpse of color dances among the tent ropes.

45

PART III
Darb Al Kunhuri (January 1961)

Again we stop atop the pebbled knoll. The Rover's motor idles, as Russ inspects the slipping fan belt. He checks security of spare gas cans braced to front fenders.

So might Ali al Ajmi detect the faltering step of a camel and arrest his caravan to pass judgment on the need. "This way, my tribesmen. Follow as I lead." But Ali has become one with the tents.

It is Russ who leads. "I'd like to locate the ruins of that fort Ali mentioned," he says to Dee. The wiped dust from hands to trousers concludes all is well with the car. "Let's pick up one of those camel trails and browse around a bit."

Beyond the As Sudayrah basin, imprints of camel hooves, shadow filled in the slanting light, record wanderings to and from the mudhole. Dee gears the truck and takes off. South. Through its rear window, I watch Cyndy's head bob with every lurch.

"If you spot anything that looks like a wall, it'll be helpful," Russ says to Linda, who rides in the Rover.

The horizon, drawn closer, reveals nothing. No crenelated battlements reminiscent of Beau Geste, to bring a brush with familiarity and shrink Arabia's unknowns. Only the slender threads of morning weave a moment akin to us into this day's passing. The truck labors through thornbush and washouts that lead nowhere. The final camel trail sifts into sand. Once I have hope of a natural roadway when the cars traverse broad layers of limestone, but nature's violence claimed its existence, and the possibility dies in the muck of a *sabkhah*. The As Sudayrah basin and its occupants, now named and therefore known to us, slip into a mirage of memory. The land is lonely emptiness, where phantom trails conceal their identity in the violet haze of yesterday.

The truck stops. "It's got me beat!" Dee calls. "Must have missed it somewhere."

Russ pulls the Rover alongside the truck. "Maybe we ought to angle west . . ."

West. Deeper into the desert. "Russ," I say. "How are we doing on gas?"

"That's my worry," he says. "Now we are going to camp." Cyndy runs up. "How about it," her father asks. "Hungry?"

"Starved!" She leaps at the door and piles herself

A long slope of clean sand and high ground invite travelers to build their *bait* for the night.

46

Crystals of calcium sulphate,
impregnated with sand,
resemble roses—buried
flowers of the desert.

onto his lap. "Can we have dinner now, Dad?"

"Sure thing."

She scrambles into the seat between us. Russ circles the car about the area before coming to rest. "We'll camp here," he says. He has selected well: high, smooth ground, hills to block the morning wind, and—"A boudoir for you, madame!"

I touch the hand of this man who has thrown his lance in front of his camel and brought his people to rest. A long light lingers in the sky, gathering its hours to be counted in the storehouse of time. We race to withhold day's final close, as Dee raises the tent, and I set savory stew bubbling on the Coleman stove. Too tired for a campfire, we respond to the need for sleep and wondering about tomorrow.

Linda and I follow the beam of Cyndy's flashlight,

as it slashes the blackness. A short distance from the tent, hunched boulders screen a finger of clean white sand. "Your boudoir," Russ had said. Yet, not ours alone. We share this privacy with others— Bedouin women before and after—all whose day's journey is stayed by stars.

An early awakening comes with the flapping of canvas walls, the scratch of the dung beetle and the chill of the sandy floor. In the solitude of pre-dawn, the Bedouin has responded to a shepherd's call: "Prayer is better than sleep." The sun replaces morning's gentleness with a brazen glare, and the passing of our cars becomes as grains of sand sweeping the wilderness.

Ahead lies a broad *sabkhah*, treacherous salt basin of the Eastern Province. Dee and Russ stand

Squatting close to the camel's
tail, the unfriendly herder
taps his mount and returns to
the herd.

at its edge, studying the surface. Salt crystals sparkle
in the slanting light. Russ thrusts a shovel into the
surface. With a crunch the blade immerses,
saturated sand oozing above the gash.

"Won't hold the cars," Russ says. "We'll have to
go back." He whistles to the girls, humped over
freshly piled ridges of tire tracks.

Linda holds out a cluster of crystalline petals
impregnated with sand. How beautiful! Flowers of
the desert—unearthed secrets of the sand. "Be
careful. They break easily," she says.

Russ plucks a formation from the pile at Linda's
feet. "Sand roses," he says. "At least that's what
ARAMCO's geologists called them."

Flower rocks, I think. Billions of years locked in
one petal. Something positive to relate to, like the

pattern of a kiss on Cyndy's boot.

"We'd better get started," Russ says.

I help gather some of the roses, dry sand spilling
from fragile petals. We pack them inside the bedrolls.
No English gardener tended his formal blooms more
carefully. An hour later, Cyndy spots a long
protrusion of layered marl encroached by a dune.

"That's got to be it!" Russ is excited. "Good girl!"
He maneuvers the Rover closer to the crumbling
wall. Its man-made layers are weathered but
distinct. Piles of debris once formed a watchtower.
Its story, carried from tent to tent, outlives the fort
itself.

Russ studies the swing of the compass, facing
south. "Now I know where I am," he says. "We're
on the right track." He speaks with assurance, as

The infinite gathers into movement, as a camel rider bounds up the slope and stares at us.

though confirming: "Last night we left Los Angeles and stayed over at Riverside. Now we'll head for San Diego . . ."

There are no names here. Where in all that debris did Russ find words? What does he seek?

"We'll head generally south," he says. "We're bound to cross it somewhere."

"Cross what?"

"An ancient caravan route. The Darb al Kunhuri that Ali told me about."

"How come Dad figures so much?" Linda asks.

"He interprets what he sees," I answer. "That makes him a leader—a *sheikh*. And also because he has luck."

"Like finding the fort?" Cyndy says.

I turn to Russ. "What is this Darb al Kunhuri?"

He tells us it was an ancient trail, well traveled, until the coastal dunes took over. No curbs nor road signs, more a feeling, a passage between Riyadh and the Najd highlands and eastward to the seaport of Jubail. Another fact labeled—more positive than the imprints of former caravans that accompany as a multitude.

In the distance, bare hills break into segments. Closer, individual buttes or small mountains rise tall, like the last guard of a regiment. *Jabal* the Arabs call them. A massive butte lies dead ahead. Here our "road" stops, as though disappearing into an Aladdin's cave. We drive the base of the barrier. At the rear we encounter a sharp drop to a *wadi* covered with *arfaj*. Camels graze in contentment, their pasture no less pastoral than a Kentucky farmland. From the rim the vista is limitless, then the infinite gathers into movement, as a camel rider bounds up the slope from the *wadi* below and stares at us.

"*Salaam alaikum* . . ." Russ calls. "What country is this?"

The herder squats atop the camel's tail, wary and uninformative. The secrets of a tribe are not to be shared with strangers. His black eyes narrow beneath a tight band of crumpled *ghutrah*, ends flagging in the breeze. His own tribesmen, appearing suddenly upon the scene, would provoke an encounter. We stand before him—strangers—a threat to the herd.

Russ steps forward. "*Ya akhuiy* . . ." But the man is no brother to us. A hiss behind clenched teeth. A flip of the hands to balance on the hump. A bound from knees to feet, and the herder stands on the

camel's back. He shakes his long stick at us, then touches the camel's neck. A stiffening tail jerks straight up; a grumble rolls through open jaws; ungainly legs slide down the incline.

"*As salaam alaikum*," Russ shouts. The peace of Allah must bid him stay. We can only speak the words. The meaning, the living of them belong to the herder, as does God's wide bounty spreading half the world before us.

"Not very friendly, that one," Dee says.

We return to the cars and drive down the shoulder of the butte. Packed sand and scraggly brush lacerate tires and torment chassis. *Dikakah* such terrain is named: tough stalks securing sand in piles, hard as dry river bottoms after flash floods have swept the valley floor. *Arfaj* abounds. The soft, grey bush rumples earth's surface to the horizon that holds the silhouettes of camels.

We see nothing to anchor the herds: no tents, no herdsmen. Only kilometers that roll behind, as others rush in ahead. The monotony is wearying. The constancy of sun and silence hypnotizes. We alone blemish space with the dust of our passing. This is an ancient wasteland, where man and his tricks are impotent.

An interruption of the monotony, as a rock striking a windshield startles the eyes and pulse. "Russ, stop!" He, too, has seen what I see: two camels and a woman—alone.

"Okay," he says. "I need to cool the engine anyway."

A moment of transition hangs over this Bedouin girl and me. It stems from the flicking of the reflex viewer, as I walk ahead: move slowly—she does not know you.

Flying yellow skirts with red roses parachute to the ground, as the girl jumps to catch a rope dangling from a camel's neck. I call out to her, then, stop—agonized. Scream after bloodcurdling scream resounds in explosive reality. Panicked, the girl lets go the rope. Her cries of terror startle the animals, and they trot off in opposite directions. Sand sprays from their hooves and from the yellow skirt that drags in flight.

Unnerved, I, too, flee—back to the cars. The Rover is already in motion. Door thrown open, I jump in with the roll. Disapproval needs no words. It's in Linda's eyes, in Russ' plunging the car straight ahead. A sense of guilt overcomes me, as Russ strives to gain distance between the car and the incident.

Russ sees what I see: two
camels and a woman—alone.

My head bangs against the roof. I grab the camera leaping off my lap.

"Do we have to go so fast?"

"You bet we do! Where there's women, there'll be men. Men intent on protecting their women and their honor . . ."

Like a reliving before disaster, recollection rushes forth: the inviolate seclusion of Muslim women, the duty of males to protect them, the barriers of custom and language, the hostile geography. Life must be lived to be known. How else but to step forward? Though now, instinctively, I glance behind.

Our dense dust cloud billows. We can never take refuge behind it. It is a beacon to all irate tribesmen —hard riding *ghazu* warriors of this day's history— curved swords unsheathed to avenge the innocent.

Russ' voice rings like an alarm. "Don't anybody get out!"

The truck pulls up to the stopped Rover. "What do you make of it?" Dee says.

Russ holds down the clutch pedal and leaves the motor running. The way ahead is blocked. Two *ghutrah* wrapped camel riders flank a third: an old man in a worn army coat, rifle raised above his head in warning.

Minutes lengthen, as the old man circles the cars. He raps the gas cans with his stick and rubs his coatsleeve on a window where our fearful eyes peer out. Helplessness rekindles fear. What about the old laws of tribal justice—are they truly non-existent? A woman's scream for a woman's scream! Oh, no! Not our daughters! I turn for a reassuring glance at them.

Cyndy is all smiles. "Exciting, isn't it?"

Linda's look says: "Well, Mom, you did it this time!"

I shift to my full sitting height. This Bedouin— this unmodernized male—he'll see how an American family meets his challenge!

But Russ just sits waiting, his hand toying with

the ignition keys, eyes scanning contours where more Bedouins might be hiding.

"What'll he do?" I whisper, not truthfully wanting an answer.

"He'll let us know when he's ready," Russ says without emotion. Then, abruptly, "You stay in the car!"

The camel's tall legs fold and refold, as the man couches his mount. The car jerks, and the motor dies. Russ gets out to meet him.

I lean across the vacated seat for a closer look. A red checked *ghutrah* swathes the Bedouin's face, exposing only his eyes, recessed and shadowed. Arabs working in oil company towns often cover their faces with a *ghutrah* for protection against wind and sand, but on this Bedouin the effect is sinister. He leans forward as he talks, raises his head and points with his stick. Light flees the shadows from his eyes, revealing white scars of trachoma. I cannot hear his words, but they are written in the wrinkles of good humor tightening about his eyes. Then, Dee's explosive laughter.

The Bedouin pulls aside his *ghutrah*. His beard is kinked and ragged—bits of wire long bent out of shape. His deeply bowed mouth stretches in a smile, companion in humor to many missing teeth. The weathered skin rises and falls in puffs of dunes about the oasis of his eyes. Dee returns to the truck and tinkers with the lock chaining a galvanized can to the slats.

"Let it go, Dee," Russ shouts. "We'll follow along with Mohammed to his tent."

"What does he want?" I ask, as we crawl along to match the camel's pace.

There is a look in Russ' eyes that says I don't deserve the only answer he can give: ". . . our sweet water for his coffee!"

Mohammed Khalifa sits his rhythmically pacing camel with the regality of a paramount *sheikh*: a tribal chieftain, leader of three thousand *bait ash sha'ar*, eight thousand camels and five thousand rifles. A man of power and influence in his desert kingdom!

Only—he isn't!

Sheikh—yes. An ageing and respected member of the clan and tribe. The old army coat is a prized possession, no less than the guile that parts us from our sweet water.

Sweet water! I go limp with relief! "Why don't you give it to him and let's go?" I ask Russ.

"Can't very well—without losing the container. Besides, I thought you'd be glad to visit another family."

I'm not all that sure. The screams still resound. There could be other men . . .

Russ interrupts my thoughts. "He's camped near the Darb al Kunhuri."

And all the while I thought we were following this elusive trail.

Linda leans forward. "How'd he know about sweet water?"

Yes—how did he? I picture that bright and shiny spigot above the kitchen sink that dispenses sweet water into homes in oil company compounds: demineralized water for drinking—product of refinery operations. The natural raw water of the Eastern Province, while non-injurious to health, is too salty to be palatable—and brews awful coffee!

Mohammed, you are no mystery—merely a human seeking comforts from life that Allah brings within reach. I have met you in many places: in the lanes of a supermarket—on a used car lot—even in the camps of ARAMCO. I am at home with you . . .

Russ interrupts my pleasurable discovery. "Don't underestimate the grapevine, nor the wits by which the Bedouin has survived for centuries."

Beyond the hills rise the *jabal*—nature's loftier tents, intruders on the sand, jagged edged and ridged. Each step near or far of them brings changes in shape, color and texture, so that to seek your way among them is to face misdirection and confusion. The whimsy of wind, rain and sun has formed toadstools, geometric balances and falcon's beak. Bold sketches drawn on a pad of clean sky. And on the desert floor, patterns of man's own making: a strip of darkened ground on yellow sand. A path that leads to life—just another mudhole of brackish water pressured to the surface by subterranean pools, and known to the tribes that come this way.

"*Lazam* (you must) give me your sweet water . . ." The echo carries the truth of Mohammed's need.

Black mounds of matted hair huddle against the blacker ground—sheep and goats waiting to be watered. I see no shepherd, no staff stuck into the ground with cloak fluttering to gather the sheep while the shepherd rests under a bush. But our cars flush activity, as flashes of brown fur, low to the ground, circle for an attack.

Mohammed's camel swings ahead, past the

Mohammed Khalifa laughs, as he parts us from our sweet water.

Another brackish pool, and a Bedu woman, containers full of water, directs her camel back to camp.

menacing dogs, the sheep, away from the pool. The Rover lurches over ground made spongey by ancient dung, sand and water. Out of nowhere a shepherd does appear: a lone figure striding across the emptiness, as we would a home town street. Mohammed hails him. The man is a cousin. All are "cousins" within a tribe.

Where is the tribal mark by which Mohammed knows him? He carries only tools of his trade: a heavy leather pouch for bringing up water, a length of coarse rope and a second bag heavy with *laban* (buttermilk) for his own use during the long hours of shepherding. With a flash of joy he recognizes Mohammed.

"*Ya akhuiy*! My brother . . . !"

Not far beyond the well, three *bait ash sha'ar* hug the stoney ground. Their walls are pinned close

to the roofs. The chill wind nags the strips of patched worsted stretched across the face of each tent. Despite the briskness of the weather, the front and rear walls of a fourth *bait* are unhooked and lie in heaps on the ground. Baby goats jump on the coarse cloth that is half buried under animal droppings, camp litter and blown sand.

Beneath the long roof, a family goes about its chores. A girl stirs a large pot in half the overhang which is the kitchen. A mother nurses her child beside the piled wall of bags and red quilts that separates two rooms. An older woman in turquoise dress layered with black veils sits at a floor loom, while another pats cheese cakes between hennaed hands and sets them on a bush to dry.

Each looks up as the cars roll into view and, startled, clasps hands to mask.

Out of nowhere a shepherd does appear, carrying the tools of his trade.

Donkeys seek protection under the tent roof, while young kids huddle against a pile of *arfaj*, placed to break the wind.

Our cars block the way of a tiny girl running to her *bait*. Wisps of hair blow from her tight *bukhnuq* (child's head covering) and catch on the gold stud ringed in her nose. Cut off from home and family, she shrieks wildly. Great tears smear the dirt on her face, and saliva drools from her trembling lips. She seems as vulnerable in this wilderness as the yellow cassia buried by the driven sand of a spring *shamal*.

Under the tent roof, cheese cakes tumble, the shuttle dives, the nursing baby sprawls in the sand, as all three women dash in front of the Rover to gather up the crying child. A furore of *abayah* (cloaks) sweeps her up—swirling guardians and protectors. The black silk of purdah. Mother of mothers. The distressed child is passed from woman to woman, each dispensing comfort and love. Which one is the mother?

A brown donkey peers past the tent, his head tassled by the overhang. A couched camel chews

disdainfully, not bothering to turn its head. The girl who stirred the pot runs after the cars and leans against a support rope, as Mohammed dismounts at the most westerly *bait ash sha'ar*.

Three boys run to greet him. They lead the camel away to be hobbled at the rear of the tent. The girl watches me, but my glance sends her away. I start to follow, as she heads for the tent where the woman weaves.

Russ cautions. "We'll do things Mohammed's way. I don't want any more problems with women!"

"I'm sure they sent the girl for me. I'd rather sit with those women than with the men."

"We're Mo's guests," Russ says. "We're invited to his tent. So watch your step. That other family is *qasir*—a tent neighbor camping for protection and not a part of Mohammed's clan."

Protocol—the right of hospitality belongs to

57

There is something about
Mohammed's *bait* that makes
you laugh.

Mohammed, for he had led us here out of the
bleakness of the desert, to rest under the shade of
his roof and to share what comforts his home
provides.

There is something about Mohammed's tent that
makes you laugh. The starkness is barely less than
the encampment of Ali al Ajmi at As Sudayrah. The
patched roof sags, but the walls surround not grim
weariness and hunger, not fear nor isolation, but
the joy of living.

Wispy bushes of *arfaj* dot the area, and racing
through them, baby goats spring like grasshoppers.
The tent itself is alive with these young animals.
They leap at the low slung walls between the poles
and up onto the roof. Unable to stand, the kids slide
the worsted slopes on sparse little rumps, like
youngsters on a slack trampoline. Children jump
and scream and catch them as they fall. The goats

kick, lunge and jump again. Mohammed joins the
fun, shaking the roof. The kids slide faster, and he
laughs louder than the children.

Such is the benevolence of Allah. Look not to
tomorrow that may bring drought and death. Live
for the joys of today—fair skies, a crisp breeze, fodder
for the animals, little ones to add to the flock, rice
and camel's milk, good health and guests to sit
about the coffee fire.

"*Ahlan—ahlan—ahlan* (welcome). The comforts
of my home are yours. What I have is yours. Now,
what is the news of the desert?"

A young man in white *thaub* and *ghutrah* steps
briskly over the dropped curtain. He is Fahd, son of
Mohammed. He holds a bowl of *laban* in outstretched
hands.

"*As salaam alaikum—sabah al khair*—peace upon
you—and the day attend you with goodness. Come

inside and be refreshed, for you have traveled far.''

Russ takes the bowl and compliments Fahd with a generous gulp of the chalky fluid. He smacks lips loudly, for enjoyment of food is lusty and audible. Fahd is delighted. How satisfying this invitation to rest, this haven in a hostile environment. But the *laban*, lightly soured camel's milk, is not to my taste, nor have I forgotten another bowl raised to the lips of a feverish child. I drink. No less a grateful guest than Russ.

We remove our shoes and enter the men's *majlis*. The sand is the same—no different from the surrounding area. Mohammed shouts across the dividing wall for *jalla* (dung fuel). Instantly, the owner of a red dress with yellow moons and stars swishes around the curtain from the women's quarters and ducks into the *majlis*. She ignores Mohammed, dumps the fuel on the ground, then pulls me toward the dividing wall. She squats, and her ringed fingers gripping my arm pull me down to sit with her. She peers at me through the slits of her mask, closing one eye, as though looking through a microscope, or focusing vision impaired by a veil. Unexpectedly, I have gained recognition. The common denominator has brought this woman and me side by side. Like the man who cried: ''*Imsh!*'', Mohammed raps the woman sharply on the back. How dare she sit! No woman remains in the *majlis* when there are guests! Deliver the fuel and—go! She dodges past him, to be showered with a tirade attached to the word: *zawjati*—my wife.

Mohammed brings the coals to life and sets the stockpot on the flickering flame. Russ settles himself against the camel saddle where Fahd joins him. This haven, barely one-third the length of the roof, is reserved for men to receive guests. The family remains behind the *qata*, the curtain that separates the two rooms. How do I fit into this formula? A guest—less honored than Russ, but somewhat raised above the station of *zawjati*, who may not stay. In the eyes of purdah, perhaps I am even less than she who keeps to the *mahram*, the sacred place.

Russ sips from the bowl of *laban*, as Fahd watches. Mohammed calls to Dee, who remains outside with the girls.

''I'll get the sweet water,'' Dee says, making a move toward the truck. His glance reveals he seeks to escape from the *laban*, but Fahd is quick to respond.

''No—later. First you must refresh yourself, by the goodness of Allah.''

''Ah, Dee,'' I think, watching him escape. ''Like Mohammed you play your own games!''

Dee hurries past the girls, away from the face of the tent, their attention drawn to Abdullah, the oldest son of Fahd. He has an orphan goat tucked under his arm. It had been sleeping inside the tent, collared by a loop of soft wool to a length of rope pegged to the ground.

''*Aish ismahu?*'' Cyndy says. ''What's its name?'' Abdullah stares at her. ''Ya Baahah.''

The little goat could be her own Siamese kitten just jumped down from the fig tree at our back door. She strokes the tiny head, creating a moment of tenderness in the swift course of life. Abdullah responds otherwise. He turns away from Cyndy's outstretched hand and tosses the animal onto the roof. Bleating, it struggles hopelessly for a footing.

''That's mean!'' Cyndy cries, in English.

Abdullah scowls at her frown. Does she not know that all creatures, human and animal, must grow strong at an early age? With his first steps, didn't he cry when the hot sand blistered his feet, and the great ball in the sky burned his back? Thirst and hunger are daily lessons, too—and the wind, that tears at the eyes and holds breath from the nostrils! Ya Baahah's legs must grow steady and his heart brave. He smiles, as he watches the struggling kid. Tonight he will wrap Ya Baahah in the red quilt to sleep with him.

Linda doesn't remember the self-determination aroused, when, as an infant, we let her cry herself to sleep. She wants to help the struggling fluff of life. Her hands grip the rough edge of the tent roof. Unexpectedly, it is torn from her grasp, as the roof erupts, sand showering down where we sit. The goat sprawls to the ground, legs flailing.

Mohammed's wife ducks from under the *bait ash sha'ar*, stick in hand, and steps over the dropped curtain of the *mahram*. I had watched her poke the roof from the inside with her camel stick and send the goats flying.

I follow Mohammed, as he dashes out. Words fly as the goats. ''Woman! You have thrown sand on my guests with your springing roof! Your stupidity dishonors my *bait*!''

''And you,'' she cries in turn. ''May your camel go lame! May you be womanless! For I must tear my fingers to the bone to repair holes in the roof!''

Mohammed slinks inside the tent.

"Let a camel's nose under the
roof, and he's all in!"

A pair of blonde camels swings quietly from behind and inches forward to the face. No one heeds them until their heads slip under the roof, provoking renewed fury from the *umm al bait* (mother of the house), as Mohammed's wife strides toward them and clouts the intruders with her stick. This time she stays and looks at me. I smile at her, appreciating the saying: "Let a camel's nose under the roof, and he's all in!" What havoc of flying tent poles, collapsed roof, trampled and strewn baggage!

Abdullah and his brothers prod the camels away. The children rap the long legs with sticks and torment the air with shouts and cries. They pound the lightly furred rumps, swing on the neck ropes, push and pull until the huge animals are down, grumbling all the way.

What an uncooperative, disgruntled beast, the camel. Not an oddity to be viewed with curiosity behind fences and bars, but the essence of life. Camels are the desert: its moods, its hardships, its poetic moments, and its turbulence. Even as I watch them go down, the disturbance they created has revolved into a crisis, for a rolling wave of lambs engulfs the second tent.

Bumped and buffeted by the piling animals, a small girl cries out, as household goods are overturned and ripped open. The boys come running. It is their *bait*—the home of Fahd. Linda and Cyndy join in the commotion. The boys push through the pack of black wool, striking out with their sticks. The central tent pole teeters, ropes squeak, saddlebags and grain sacks tumble. Now goats join the melée.

Lambs swirl inside the tent like lumps of cheese stirred in a bowl of clotting milk.

"Abdullah!" Linda shouts. "Get that one!" She doesn't know how to stop the jumping animals, springing from the *qata* wall.

A young woman rescues Ya Baahah from the turmoil and stands watching. The hubbub of shouts overrides the gentle voice of Fahd, who stands beside me.

"My sons," he says. "Abdullah, the oldest. Then Ahmed, and Salim." He is amused at the near disaster to his *bait*. But it is not his concern: the women and children take care of the tent. Such events occur every day. The boys handle the sheep— the women clean up the mess.

"My father is asking for you," he says. "Honor his house with your presence." He escorts me back

Abdullah and his brothers
chase the milling sheep from
their *bait*.

Hussa demands a second five
riyal for Ya Baahah.

to the *majlis*.

Mohammed bids me sit on the far side of the
camel saddle. He drops the curtain, lest the tent
neighbor see the pot bubbling and Mohammed be
duty bound to invite him in. The dung coals glow
brightly. Smoke whirls about the broad beaked pot,
caked with ash as black as the walls. The long
handled spoon and rake for roasting the coffee beans
lie idle on the sand. Coffee is a luxury. Today coffee
will not be made fresh. We shall drink what is left
in the stockpot.

And the sweet water? Mohammed will not accept
it until we have shared food in his *bait*.

Later, the opportunity comes for me to meet other
women of the family—those who direct their efforts
and responsibilities toward the good of the whole.
Her name is Hussa, and she is thirteen years old.

She stands at her brother Fahd's tent, holding the
baby goat, as the stampede subsides. Yes, she
answers my question, the child Farida is sister to
the boys. Their mother is dead, taken by Allah when
Salim was born. Now she, Hussa, youngest sister to
the father is mother to the children. She may not
marry, but will keep her brother's tent and take
care of his children as long as he remains without
a wife.

Hussa is not unhappy. There are no male cousins
for her to marry, and she would not want to leave
her family for a husband from another tribe. One
day she may have to, if her parents so decide. She
holds the baby goat against her veiled cheek. Not
much older than Linda—yet, dedicated to duty and
responsibility.

I offer her a five *riyal* note to spend on the next

Life defies the desert's
hardships, for Amsha carries
a seed within herself.

trip to the village for supplies. "*Khamsah* (five) *riyal*—for you."

She takes the money and hides it in an inner pocket of her cloak. Her eyes sharpen. "*Ashrah!*" she demands. "*Lazam ashrah riyal!*"

"Ten *riyal?*" I question, wondering at her ungratefulness.

"Yes—you must!" she says, holding up ten fingers.

"Five for you—no more."

Her demand is intense. "No! You must! *Khamsah riyal* for Hussa. *Khamsah riyal* for Ya Baahah!" She extends the goat.

Like her father Mohammed, she misses no opportunity. The ten *riyal* disappear into the folds of Hussa's cloak, and she leaves, as Mohammed's wife approaches. A firm grip on my arm and excited chattering direct me into the *mahram*.

A palm mat covers the floor where I sit with Mohammed's family. Enjoying them all, I am suddenly sobered at the presence of one young woman. It is not a game, this living in tents, but the pursuance of existence in all its realities. Life's continuance defies the mudhole. A hidden seed challenges next year's drought. It will grow and change as the eternal shifting of sands. And, "*Inshallah!*" (by the will of Allah), it will see dawn and survive.

Children. Creation clinging to a weathered tent. And I am one with this Bedouin woman who bears life within herself. She is Amsha, wife of Mohammed's brother Ali, who has taken camels to market.

Amsha is happy to be bearing another child. Children are wealth, hands to help, prestige for family and tribe. It is indeed Allah's blessing that brings children. She picks up a roly-poly child and stands it on her knee.

"A boy?" I ask.

Her eyes brighten. She lifts the child's dress so there can be no doubt. We laugh. It is a good secret. And my suspicions are confirmed: Bedouin babies wear no diapers! The small girl in the high peaked bonnet is Amsha's, too. But, hopefully, the new baby will be another son.

Where will it be born? Likely the first anguish will stir on the march, and Amsha will stop alongside the camel trail to give birth. What will the baby be named? Abdullah, perhaps, as the servant of God. Nura, for light, or Musbubah,

meaning pouring out, if the birth is easy. But her agony will be great if the womb was packed with salt after the other births, thus hardening and destroying the elasticity of the tissues. Perhaps she will reach a village where there is a Government Clinic.

Behind the mask, Amsha's eyes are tranquil. She gathers the little girl in her arms and brushes strands of hair from the face. The child is listless—ill, no doubt, for pneumonia strikes many children during the winter months. The dark eyelashes are stuck with pus, and Amsha dabs at it with her skirt. Her veil falls forward as she leans, revealing a turquoise nose stud, and a touch of blue on a string woven into her hair. I reach out to confirm my understanding of its identity. She ducks from my hand.

"*Shuf* (look), that's all," I say. "It is very pretty."

She allows me to touch her hair, henna tinted. To finger the medallion dangling on its string. I turn it over. The blue enameled likeness of the Virgin Mary binds me to this woman's life, so alien to my own.

Amsha explains that a lady doctor at the Buraimi Oasis gave it to her when her first child died. It will protect the children.

I have a touch of blue, too. I take the bell bracelet with its turquoise bead from my pocket and put it on my arm. If I asked a computer what a touch of blue has to do with the welfare of a child, it would not have been programmed to respond. The answer lies in the trust of Amsha, in the footsteps of the camel, in the clip clop of a donkey on its way to David's City.

The men remain in the *majlis*, Mohammed stirring the coals at the edge of the roof. The dust from churned sand has settled, and Hussa and the children—Fahd's and mine—are looping the lambs. Cyndy runs to me. I get up to smooth her tangled hair, and the bracelet jingles.

"*Wajid zain.* Very good," Mohammed says, as he appears beside me and reaches for the bells.

I remove the bracelet, thinking he may tell me its origin. His gnarled fingers grab the circlet from my hand and shake it. He grins broadly, eyes narrowing with devilish delight. His voice augments the sound of the tinkling bells, calling the camp children to gather round, *al abu* (father) has a new game for them to play! Mohammed dodges, as Abdullah, Farida and little Salim chase after him.

Mohammed runs off, the bell
bracelet dangling over one ear.

"I'd keep an eye on that old duck," Dee says, stepping out from the *majlis*. "In fact, I think I'll see what he's up to."

Mohammed emerges from behind the tent, goats and children racing after him. He holds up his arms, eyes round with glee. He shakes both wrists, wiggles all ten fingers. No sound of bells. The children clamber over him, searching.

The bracelet is gone.

Mohammed takes off again, and Linda follows him. He squats behind the tripod where the waterskins hang. The faint ringing of bells sends the children in search of *al abu*. With a whoop of delight Mohammed jumps up and reveals the bracelet encircling one ear. Abdullah cannot reach it. Mohammed will not allow Linda to come near. The children lose interest. The game is over.

Swift as a fox Mohammed speeds to the women, who squat just inside the *bait*. Linda follows, watching, as he stoops near Amsha.

"*Minfadlak* (please), give me the bracelet," Linda says, holding out her hand.

He looks at her. "*Aish* (what)?" He feigns surprise, turns on her, and walks away.

"Why—that old goat!" Dee says.

"He's hidden it in that child's dress!" Linda is angry.

"Yes—I saw him!" Cyndy says.

I want to call Russ, but the probabilities of the situation bear down on me. To confront Mohammed —to insult the women by a search? Several times the hand of a thief has hung on the Dhahran Main Gate after a severing. The crime is not in the stealing, but in getting caught. Do I wish desert justice to gather in a *bait ash sha'ar*, the elders and the *ulema* (religious men) to decide whether I have been wronged? Better I lose a circlet of bells than Mohammed. . . . Still—in my world I do not want to lose. I face Amsha. Her eyes remain blanks. She sits unmoving, but as the baby rolls on her lap, I detect a tinkle of bells muffled by the sack of sweet herbs tied around its neck.

"Never mind, Mom," Linda says. "It is your bracelet—why don't we just take it?"

In the press of my fingers against her own, does she sense that the bracelet with its blue bead is merely a symbol, its value determined within ourselves? "No," I say. "It doesn't matter that much."

I have not swallowed the bitter liquid from salted wells, suffered the gnaw of hunger, faced each day knowing death is never very far away. How, then to censure a moment of fun in life's uncertainty, or Mohammed's need to acquire for his family what his wits will win? The interaction of humans has skillfully bypassed thousands of years.

There is much we have to learn of this desert. Even now, its story further unfolds, for a camel herd comes into view, swinging across the desolation. Together, Linda and I hurry past the *qasir* tent to meet it. Dee joins us.

"I've been watching that old duffer out there," he says. A solitary camel rider approaches the encampment from the opposite direction of the arriving herd.

"Who do you suppose he is?"

"Mohammed says the man camped with them a few nights ago. Said he was going north—back to his tribe, the Awazim."

"Strange, how he keeps getting on and off his camel—riding in circles," I say.

"Probably looking for something he lost," Dee says.

For the tenth time the stranger mounts his camel, rides a few paces, couches his beast, gets off and walks, the camel following. All the while, the man inspects the ground at his feet. In such manner he

Mohammed's family daily
faces the rigors of Bedouin life.

The walls of a cave are
marked with tribal insignia
—like *wasm*, brands put on
camels and the
casements of wells.

covers a wide area between Mohammed's tents and
the base of a large *jabal*. Now, the lone shepherd we
passed earlier appears, as if from nowhere. The
stranger accosts him.

"The way Bedouins pop up around here, I bet that
guy'll never find what he lost," Linda says.

"Not so," Dee says. "My Saudi crew boys tell me
no tribesman will touch anything found on the
desert. It will be there when the owner returns."

"Humph!" Cyndy says, who has joined us. "Not
with Mohammed around!"

"Well—tricks are one thing. Stealing another,"
Dee tells her. "Besides, your mother didn't have her
wasm on that bracelet."

"*Wasm?* What's that?" Linda asks.

"Now, sprout, you don't know?" Dee laughs.
"Well, I'll tell ya . . . it's your tribal mark—your
tribal signature . . ."

"I know," Cyndy says. "Like a coat-of-arms."

"I wouldn't say that, exactly," Dee explains.
"That's too fancy. Mostly circles and lines—like a
Texas cattle brand. Didn't you see them on the
camels?"

"Hey, no!" Cyndy says. "Come on—show me,
Dee!" She drags him away to mingle with the
activity of the arriving herd.

Linda's interest focuses on a young girl standing
in front of the *qasir* tent. The girl stares intently at
the lone camel rider, who draws closer to the
encampment. The even features of her face are
uncovered, and she scowls at us, as though unhappy
at our presence. The shout of a woman startles her,
and she turns toward the hubbub of the milling
herd.

The woman has jumped down from her camel
and is calling to the children. "You, Selma—

The strange Bedouin leads his
camel in circles, as if searching
for something he has lost.

Selma stares after the lone
rider, little knowing what's in
store for her.

Hammid—help with the camels! You, Ali and
Wafa—get the hobbles. Abdullah, Farida—tie the
milk camels behind the tent! Ahmed, Salim—bring
the young ones to feed from their mothers!" She
strides toward the tent, her blowing skirts of the
same material as the dresses of Amsha and
Mohammed's wife.

The girl in front of the *qasir* tent moves to join the
running children. A rough, high knuckled hand
clamps her shoulder. A woman emerging from the
tent has observed everything.

"*La* (no), Selma! Leave the camels to the others.
You fetch the water, blow the coals . . ." With a
shove of both hands, she pushes the girl inside the
tent.

For a minute the woman reviews the scene,
paying strict attention to the lone rider. A passing
glance at me, and she follows Selma into the tent.
Loud voices are raised in dispute. A second woman
drags a saffron curtain from off the wall of stored
goods and deftly hooks it to the roof. It settles down,
shutting the interior from view.

The first woman returns. Again she watches the
camel rider. He comes within range of the camp and

dismounts. The men stand waiting for him.

"*As salaam alaikum . . .*"

"*Wa alaikum as salaam.*" (And peace be upon
you.)

I respond to a sharp tap on my shoulder. Fist to
her veiled face, the *qasir* woman beckons me inside.
Again a darkly hennaed hand nudges me. The cuff
of its green dress is densely stitched in loops of
work-worn thread, once gold. Linda and I step
through the drawn gap in the curtain. A girl shakes
a square of matting and spreads it for us to sit on.
She scurries back to the shadows behind the *maksar*.
It is Selma, her fringe of curly hair and petulant lips
hidden behind a mask. How abruptly comes the
termination of childhood.

There are others in the tent: younger children, an
infant, an old woman, who squats beside an orange
teapot balanced on a circle of ash encrusted stones.
Her knobby fingers grasp a section of skirt to fan the
coals, which come to life in a spiral of smoke and
flame.

Linda stares through the frame of the *maksar* at
the troubled eyes of Selma. What can Selma know of
Linda's juke boxes and volleyball? Or, Linda know

68

The old woman makes tea in
an ash encrusted pot.

of Selma's way of locating a hidden rainpool, finding
a lost camel? Time and environment produce great
differences. In the desert, all are equal—but we are
not of the desert.

"*Tafaddali* (be comfortable). *Ahlan wa sahlan*
(welcome)." The *qasir* woman is eager to
communicate. I respond to her question.

"This is my daughter, Linda. And Selma is your
daughter? No, I have no sons."

"*Inshallah*—Allah will bring sons. Grandsons! I
am called Muna." She hands a packet of tea to the
old woman, then reaches behind her for tiny glasses
wrapped in a rag of striped cloth. "Ya, Selma—more
coals!"

From the *qash* (the wall of sorted goods), Selma
dumps dung on a tray and drops it by the fire. A
cloth ornamented with shells and colored woollen
tassels decorates the top of the wall. Linda asks me
what it is, but I don't know, so I ask. Muna tells
Linda to sit on the saddle that supports the high
hoops of the *maksar* and tosses the cloth canopy
over the hoops. It is pounded camel hide, pliant and
soft. A shower of sand douses Linda's hair, and we
laugh, as she peeks out of this desert carriage.

"Allah! Allah!" Muna cries. "She is so ugly!"

Instantly, Linda clamps her lips to conceal her
dental brace.

"Ayii—ayii!" Muna moans. "For the husband to
raise the veil on the wedding night!"

The moment is here to ask what I would know.
"Selma is very pretty. Why do you cover her face?"

"She must. It is time." Muna looks at Linda, and
in terms of the life she has to deal with, indicates my
daughter's head should be covered, too.

The old woman serves tea: hot, light and heavily
sugared. It is refreshing, equalizing, conducive to
conversation. Muna tells us the stranger met Selma
among the camels—now he brings trouble for the
family. His tribe is weak, and Selma is promised to
her *ibn al amm* (first cousin). She must remain with
the women.

This moment of Selma's anxiety communicates
without words. It deepens with the rustle of skirts,
the click of the kettle on the stones, the sputter of
arfaj in the coals, the indrawn breath that sucks up
tea beneath the lifted veil. Outside, the shrillness of
children's voices. Selma is a child no more.

"I, too, am a stranger," I say.

"No," Muna says. "You are family—*aiyal*. You
come with the blessings of Allah."

As Ali made of us cousins to share a mare.

The loom stands on empty Gee cans alongside the
maksar. Muna straddles the warp strings, the shuttle
thread held taut between her toes. I watch, as she
moves the long slender stick that serves as a shuttle
in and out of the threads. She fingers the layer of
veils on her chest, finds a gazelle horn hanging on a
string, and pushes down the woven strand of wool.
She invites me to try. I cannot squat and extend one
leg to hold the yarn as she does. She is amused that
I give up so readily.

Muna picks up a bowl, throws back the saffron
curtain, and steps outside. Our eyes wince at the
glare, settling into violet haze against the *jabal*. The
cool air freshens the warmth of the tent. We must
be leaving soon, though the comfort within worsted
walls bids me stay.

A commotion behind the tent startles me:
women's voices raised in argument, the slosh of
water, a crowd gathering. The old woman at the tea
fire picks herself up and follows Selma outside. The
young children run, and we follow. Behind us, the
infant cries in its hammock.

Muna holds her bowl, now filled with water.
Nearby, a woman in a red dress with moon and stars
breathes loudly, her clothes disheveled, her fists
clenched. She rushes Muna and slaps the bowl from
her hands. With a cry, Muna pounces upon her
attacker, forcing her backwards until the woman
trips over the tent ropes and sprawls flat on the
ground with a gasp. Muna laughs, retrieves her
bowl, brushes the sand off with her skirt, and pours
more water from a goatskin.

I recognize the attacker as Mohammed's wife.
She gets to her feet, adjusts her mask so she can see,
grabs two fistfuls of sand, and, running, throws the
sand into Muna's bowl of water. Now the fight is on
in earnest. The combatants strike and pound each
other: pushing, yelling, and tripping over their own
skirts. The crowd of women laughs and cheers. No
one interferes.

Skirts torn, veils flying, masks askew so neither
can see, the combatants tangle with each other.
Surreptitious glances and giggles from onlookers
come my way. What has provoked this attack?
Never in my life have I seen women fight—except in
the movies! Mohammed's wife gets a stranglehold
on Muna's neck and forces her backwards. She falls
in a tangled heap of skirts and veils. The crowd
cheers. Mohammed's wife straightens her clothes

70

Ahmed, Farida, little Samira,
Abdullah, Hussa and Amsha
watch the fight between Muna
and Mohammed's wife.

Fahd poses for the camera
with two of the tent children.

and walks toward her tent with dignity.

Embarrassed, we seek Russ. Why had
Mohammed's wife come to pick a fight with her
tent neighbor? I am certain it concerns us. Russ had
warned: don't get mixed up with the *qasir* tent.

Linda and I join Russ and Fahd. They study the
infinity of desert, as Fahd points the way of the Darb
al Kunhuri. No track, no marker, nothing familiar.
One traverses the remembrance of others who
passed before.

"Come. I shall take you," Fahd says. He lifts Salim
into his arms more tenderly than Amsha her child.
I reach out and touch the child's cheek. "You would
like a picture?" Fahd says.

I click the shutter again and again. Fahd poses
with the children, the donkey, the baby animals—
even the little white kid, forever to be remembered
as "*Khamsah Riyal*". He walks me to the car, the
children following, and stands close to me as I open
the door.

"*Tafaddali . . .*" (please) he says quietly, averting
my face. An object slips from his hand into mine—
the bell bracelet.

Abruptly, Fahd strides toward Russ. "You must
promise to return! We will kill a sheep! You will
know the true hospitality of the desert!"

Dee drags a can of sweet water from the truck bed.
"Hey, Mohammed! Come get your sweet water!"

Mohammed pours the water into a goatskin.
What did it take to retrieve the bracelet? Not in
effort, but in loss of honor? Mohammed doesn't
seem concerned. Fahd has taken over the
reparations for his cupidity, for the stockpot, Hussa's
"*Khamsah Riyal*", the fighting women.

"You must return! We will kill a sheep!"

Sensitivity shouts with his words: do not leave
me lost in my own faults, restore the honor of self,
erase the stigma of meanness from my family.

But we cannot return. Even should we find this
way again, Mohammed and his family would be
gone.

The curling smoke of a campfire, released from
its source, dissipates into nothing. So the Bedouin
encampment fades with distance. The churning
dust of our passing sets up an impenetrable screen,
pushing us farther into the unrestrained hostility
of the land.

"Dad, did you see those women fighting?" Linda
says.

"Yes. That's your mother for you!"

"What did I do?"

"Got Mohammed all upset because you went into
the *qasir* tent."

"But—we were invited."

"Of course you were. And you got emotional. You
didn't listen to what I told you. Mohammed had the
only right to us as guests. He was also honor bound
to respect his tent neighbor. He couldn't do anything
about your walking off to the neighbor's tent."

So clear—now. Mohammed's wife defended her
husband's rights in the only way she knew—picked
a fight and won!

This arid, inhospitable land bears life in the trust
of Amsha, the chivalry of Fahd, the defense of
family honor.

Cyndy pounds my shoulder. "Did you see that
big bird?" She rubs dust from the window.

I see the fading blue of the sky, the shimmer of
the sun's trembling descent, the blurring of *jabal*,
the greying of white limestone, the eternal sand piled
against desert brush.

"Hardly a bird out there," Russ says. He is tired.
I can tell. It takes skill and concentration to hold
those wheels.

Cyndy huffs: "And I suppose that wasn't a car I saw, either!"

"We all know Dee's truck is ahead," Linda says, for Fahd rides the lead with Dee.

But Cyndy's bird is real, and so is the car—and perhaps even the Darb al Kunhuri! A few kilometers ahead we intersect a rutted course of churned up sand with high side drifts. It swerves back toward the direction from which we have come, and its yellowness separates from the dark brush, as it wanders distantly ahead over rolling hills.

A pickup is stalled, buried to its hub caps. Dee has stopped, and we follow suit, as Fahd greets several men lounging about the truck. Back some distance from the cars, two rows of falcons perch on stools staked into the sand. We have come across a hunting party from Qatar, a sheikhdom that juts like a thumb into the Arabian Gulf.

These majestic birds of powerful plumage wear tailored hoods of white kid leather and sit on cushioned seats, brass studded and brilliant of hue. Lords of the desert—sightless to all but prey.

And the hunters are just as exciting with their gauntlets, guns and bandoliers! Unexpectedly, the desert displays a dimension beyond survival: an arena for sportsmen. The men are seeking bustard, a wild turkey-like bird.

Russ offers them the winch. The Sheikh is amused at our dependence on the mechanical, at the vulnerability of wheeled transportation. That the car won't move is of small concern. Self reliance conquered the desert long before the coming of the automobile.

The Sheikh's eye is keen as the eye of the bird. He sees how the small American girl watches the falcons: eager, expectant. His command is straight and swift of flight. A hunter responds, touching his gauntleted arm to the breast of a falcon. Taloned feet step onto the gauntlet, digging into the thick leather. The bird's great wings spread and beat in anticipation, as the tether is freed.

The hood is off! Eyes pierce the glare. The head circles on ruffled feathers. The hooked beak opens and shuts with a hiss. Talons tighten. The hunter tosses the falcon into the air. Powerful wings carry the bird up, then dive into the brush. A brief scuffle. A rise of dust, and the bird returns—a small hare shivering in its talons.

"For you, my friend," the Sheikh says, extending the bleeding, squealing creature to Russ.

"Allah rewards the skill of the hunter," he says. "The prize is rightfully yours to enjoy."

I do not appreciate the finesse of Russ' use of Arabic, but the Sheikh does. He is not insulted by the return of his gift in the name of Allah's goodness.

"My brother, the Amir of Qatar, invites you to be his guests," he says.

"And we shall come, *inshallah*," Russ answers. "And now—can you tell me of the Darb al Kunhuri?"

At last the ancient caravan route comes to life. It has names: Jubail—'Uwaynah—Ma'aqala—Dahna—Riyadh. Pinpoints of life in the wilderness.

Chanting in unison, the hunting party lifts the pickup and carries it to firm ground. With good humor they pack the birds inside, and then all pile in, even finding room for Fahd, since they are returning in his direction.

We all shout "*Ma assalamah!*" (goodbye) to the men, the birds and Fahd, as the pickup takes off in a shower of sand. Russ follows the Sheikh's directions of "over there" to a turn off, now certain to find the Darb al Kunhuri, Jubail and Ras Tanura at last.

Fatigue settles on us, weary and strained from the grinding of the motor and the lurch of wheels. A chill replaces the sun's declining warmth, and the girls wrap up in their sleeping bags. The close of this long day is slow in coming. The light hangs in the sky, as though it would never rest. Confusing patterns distort the contour of the ground, and we lose the ability to determine a thoroughfare. Russ and Dee rally for a consultation.

"I'm going to take a wild guess," Russ says. "We're too far north—maybe heading toward Jabal An Nu'ayriyah."

An Nu'ayriyah is the northernmost installation of the oil company, exclusive of the Tapline compounds, and first of a system of pump stations that keeps the oil flowing through the cross country pipeline on its way to the Mediterranean port of Sidon. Here the blacktop of the Northern Access Road ends.

"Don't recognize it from this direction," Dee says. He peers through the haze. "But I sure would know that radio tower if I saw it! Hate to tell you how many times I've climbed that thing—all two hundred feet of it! Never could get my Saudi crew to do it . . ."

Dee and the red truck take the lead. We hold to

A hunter persuades a falcon
onto his gauntlet.

We watch Dee's red truck
disappear, knowing the desert
is now ours alone.

the compass and to the intuition of the drivers,
trying to sight an oasis, a bed of lava rock and
above all the radio tower of An Nu'ayriyah.

Russ speeds through pockets of soft sand trapped
about loose limestone that rips up tires. Without
warning a terrific blow jolts the undercarriage of the
Land Rover. I feel the impact beneath my feet. Death
throes seem to shake every rotating mechanism.
Russ rolls the car to a stop.

On inspection, Russ finds the undercarriage to be
in good shape. He walks back to the point of impact
and finds an old car spring half buried in the sand.
Our wheels had caught one end of it, sending the
bar leaping upwards. There must be damage from
such an instrument. A deep and shiny gash shows
on the differential, inches from being a totally
crippling blow. Russ drives the car ahead and stops

by the waiting truck. Together the men assess the
damage.

"I smell gas," Dee says.

Dull and sticky sand crud coats the gas tank,
sharpening a glistening abrasion of metal along the
seam. The tank has been struck, and the seam
strained. The odor of gasoline is strong.

Now the cars stay close together. The fumes of
gasoline intensify, and the needle gauge drops fast.
Every jolt threatens to rupture the damaged seam.
We await the moment when the tank's life blood
will gush out on the sand.

Dee brings the truck to a stop. "Think that's our
jabal over yonder."

"If it is, Dee, we're not so badly off," Russ replies.
"But I can't make that distance on the gas I've got
left . . ."

The lone Bedouin moves on, but somehow I feel he will not be very far away.

A decision. Dee will go ahead in the truck. If that *jabal* is An Nu'ayriyah, he'll fill up with gas and come back. We watch the red truck disappear into the haze, knowing that the desert is now ours alone . . .

Cautiously, the Rover limps along. The sun begins to slip below the horizon. Dee's sand tracks, once filled with shadow, now fade into flatness: a fragile trail to follow. As one, we realize the awesomeness of the tracks' disappearance over a stretch of black basalt.

"Do you think Dee is there yet?" Cyndy speaks of our growing anxiety.

"Not likely," her father says. "But we can keep going if we pick up his tracks again."

The girls and I leave the car. We spread across the basalt, all within sight of each other. The evening breeze flutters the hair, its touch more hospitable than the one at dawn. Am I accepting this land? More willing to cope than to be afraid? Trusting in the caring of He who sees all?

The slick, black basalt reveals no impression of tires. We are not trackers of the desert to read the meaning of a dislodged pebble, a turned stone. Russ whistles us to return.

Cyndy's voice holds no expectance, only weariness, as she says: "There's a man over there. He looks like he's praying . . ."

Her sighting is not questioned, and shortly a camel rider comes into view, leading a string of four young camels. Russ takes no chances. He impounds us in the car.

The Bedouin brings encouragement. There are tracks of a heavy car beyond the basalt bed. And, yes, Jabal An Nu'ayriyah is—over there. He offers his camels to show us the way. What good are wheels, when Allah bids them not to go?

"We are all right," Russ says. "Our wheels will go." We, too have laws of the desert: never travel at night, and never leave your stranded vehicle.

The lone Bedouin moves on to meet the darkness, but somehow I carry the feeling he will not be very far away. Russ turns on the ignition and presses the throttle. With a cough and a choke the engine dies. We settle down to wait.

Thin, grey shadows thicken about the bushes, and black pits form under every stone and curve. Objects grow in stature, as the sun's residual reflection plays a final game. Alone in the growing darkness, we wait—as many a Bedouin family has waited throughout the endless centuries: they for probabilities—we for the assurance that comes with sight of a winking red light atop a radio tower, tiny and insecure in the vastness and half-light before darkness.

PART IV
"Shamal!" (April 1961)

A BEDOUIN LOVE SONG
Hail to those days when I used
To live near my loved ones,
My laughter among them during
My childhood turned later into
Crying when they went away.
A brave was I; they defeated me.
A strong was I; they captivated me
Wish I could free myself
Of their yoke!

An Nu'ayriyah—outpost of technology! Sudden greenness of peepul trees, dusty pink of oleanders, crab grass fronting white *burasti*, the portable housing for company employees. Cement block sheds with tin roofs confine the roar of diesel engines energizing gargantuan pumps.

Technology, like the Bedu, seeks water. Here, the promise of life's continuance stands high on a tripod of steel. Not a mudhole, but a watertank, its aluminium paint silver in the sun. This moment of re-entering the familiar, records Muna's weathered hands preparing the day's *laban*, as she rocks a goatskin of camel's milk roped to a tripod of *sidr* sticks. Did she pass this way, hear the engines roar louder than the clash of thunderheads, and move on—An Nu'ayriyah's existence irrelevant to her life?

A handful of cardboard shacks clusters behind the pump station gates, and fringing them—a gas station! One lone pump, hand operated, on a cement slab. A swayback metal chair, tilted on bandy legs, houses the attendant. Goats scatter raising dust, heads and tails flung upwards in surprise, as we drive up. The one time herdsman rises slowly, his loose *thaub* oil spattered. The man and his new skills are unmatched. He bobs awkward as the goats, with each turn of the handle. But I welcome the whoosh

of gasoline flowing into the Rover's tank, vapor rising like a newly donned veil.

Technology. The beginning of commercialism. Oil. I am these, too.

I relish each inch of the radio tower, guardian of our night, and treasure its ruby light, now less brilliant than the day. Return to the desert, you patterns of camel trails—you dragging skirts skittering the smooth sand! I have no need for you now, you ripples in a rainpool!

We hurry to the recreation hall within the oil company compound. A refreshing washup: hot water! No more a basinful behind a bush, or a cleaning with sand. Then a rush to savor the tantalizing aromas of bacon frying and warm sugar rolls fresh from the oven.

And, after that—the blacktop. No more to wonder where we are. The man-laid roadway knows where it is going. Tired and sore, yet revitalized, we ride out the Rover's long limp to Ras Tanura, the red truck close behind. The expanding desert, changing

We called it "Ash Sheikh"—the enormous dune that guided the traveler long before the coming of the Northern Access Road.

Did Muna pass this way with her camel herd, hear the engines roar and move on, the oil pump station irrelevant to her life?

from brush to dunes to *sabkhah*, the distant herds of camels are no longer our concern, as An Nu'ayriyah's pump station is not Muna's. The Bedu slip into their ancient past, for we are headed home.

Five hours of driving bring into view two rows of rusty oil drums that line the final turn onto the Ras Tanura headland. The blacktop parallels quadruple rows of pipelines, the township of Rahimah, the oil dump. Then the sign above the Main Gate: "Ras Tanura—Home of Safety".

Russ slows the Rover to a stop between the high wire gates. A Saudi Arab security guard, neat in khaki uniform and checkered *ghutrah*, steps from the gatehouse. "Glad you not lost, sahib," he says, handing Russ the log book.

Russ shoves his ten gallon hat to the back of his head and rubs the crease along the hairline. He signs in as having returned safely, though late.

"Get my message, Jassim?" he asks.

"Yes. Mr. Dee telephoned from An Nu'ayriyah last night. Said you coming in today." Jassim looks the Rover over, including the bedraggled occupants. "Car okay now?" Jassim's question reflects the

Saudi Arab's first acquaintance with the automobile. He accepted it without question, but, that a car didn't run when it was supposed to aroused astonishment.

"Guess what," Cyndy says. "We saw some falcons—and a Bedouin helped us."

"I don't go to the desert, Miss Cyndy," Jassim shakes his head. "The Bedu are not good people. Better you stay in Ras Tanura."

We drive along Arabian Gulf Boulevard, the one thoroughfare of our town by the sea. Machines buzz from the workshops. Great tankers line up at the bulk plant. The flare from the refinery curls upwards in immense rolls of smoke and flame, its long shadow creeping across the land where caravans once traveled.

In front of the Commissary—the company food store—Saudi employees in native dress help brief-skirted western housewives load bags of groceries into taxis. Women do not drive cars. Jasmine hedges, two tall palm trees and flowering bougainvillaea climbing a *jareed* (dried palm spine) fence greet our approach to House 2704. I luxuriate in the security of being home. Once again I am part of this Stateside Community, miraculously transplanted on the edge of the past, however small and confined it appears now.

The Rover swings into the alley and pulls up under the date palms. A *jareed* fence encloses a patio and back door. Ahmad, our Yemeni houseboy, rushes to unload the car.

"Why did Jassim say that about the Bedouins?" Linda asks her father.

Russ drags a sleeping bag from the rear of the car.

"The Bedu used to plunder pilgrim caravans and raid each other's camps." He tosses her the bedroll.

Linda takes the bag, unrolls it, and sets a cluster of sandroses on the grass. "I thought Ibn Saud changed all that."

"Can't do it overnight," Russ says. "Some Bedouins settled, but most are still on the desert, and the old stories get retold."

Linda was only eight months old when the great warrior king, who gave his name to a kingdom, drove past her baby buggy on the streets of Dhahran. How exciting it was to see him: Ibn Saud, the Sheikh of Sheikhs, champion of the tribes, blessed with unwavering faith, undaunted spirit, luck, and—oil.

Unloading is but the first step in a follow-up period that lasts several weeks. The local junk shops of Al Khobar—once a village of fishermen, now showing signs of urban development—fail to turn up a replacement gas tank. The oil company's Reclamation Yard announces its dissection of worn out vehicles for salvable parts, and Russ comes home in triumph. The transplant proves a complete success, and provides an even larger capacity for gas. Next, tires are removed and tested, screws and bolts tightened over every inch of the chassis, gas and water lines checked for dust blockage, fan belt for desiccation. Until, once again, washed and shining (if sandpapered paint can shine!), the *"Jarbu"* champs beneath the palm trees, sporting Cyndy's gift of gaudy paper flowers wired to the antenna.

One Friday in April—the Muslim holy day and our weekend—we decide to take the Rover out for a test run.

"Let's go to Ash Sheikh," I say.

Ash Sheikh—the enormous dune on the Northern Access Road—a golden beacon that guided the traveler long before the thin black line of asphalt injected change into the centuries.

The Rover purrs at 90 kilometers per hour along the Dhahran-Ras Tanura road. To the left spreads the deep green of the Qatif Oasis, former haven for Arabian Gulf pirates. High casements stand above thousand year old wells, and tiny hamlets hug the base of a deteriorating Turkish Fort. The Jawan Tomb sits on an escarpment to the right, discovered during the bulldozing for a quarry in the construction years of ARAMCO. Erected in the form of a cross with treasures and burial sites intact, its discovery enriched the history of the Eastern Province.

A small whitewashed building appears on the left. A line of oil drums leads to a single, hand-operated gasoline pump. With the completion of each successive strip of the Northern Access Road, trucks and lorries struggle along its ragged route hauling cargo from Lebanon, Iraq and Kuwait. During the Hajj season, the station stands guard over the eastern gateway to Makkah. More than once we have encountered streams of buses rolling bumper to bumper along the Access Road. Forty from Turkey. Sixty-five from Lebanon. Fifty from Iraq. Pilgrims no longer face months of hardship on camelback, but stifling weeks in crowded buses. The vehicles stop in long, sagging lines, spewing their weary loads onto the ground—to pray, to make

coffee, and wrapped in heavy *bisht* (men's cloaks), to sleep on the cold sand.

Today the road is ours. We turn right at the intersection of the Northern Access Road and the Ras Tanura Road. Two kilometers farther we make another sharp right onto a kind of causeway that crosses vast expanses of salt encrusted marl—the surface topping of treacherous, oozing sand that forms the *sabkhah* of the Eastern Province. The hard packed road rises above the mire, where pools glisten like mica in the morning sun. Beyond the *sabkhah* to the right marches the backside of the coastal dunes, whose slip faces, pointing east, are a familiar sight on the Ras Tanura Road. Here the wind is blowing hard. A yellow sky tosses its burden of flying sand, and the paper flowers are ripped off the antenna.

"Looks like a *shamal* coming up," I say. "Think we ought to turn back?"

"Heck no, Mom." Cyndy says. "We haven't come to the dune yet."

The months of March and April bring violent winds from the northwest that sweep sand at gale force across the land. For weeks on end they blow, blinding and choking, laying veils of dust over everything and building small dunes, inside and out, against any core that provides an anchor. Not only yellow dust, but burnt orange—from the red sands of the Great Nafud Desert to the north—so that our town appears curtained by billows of flame.

"We'll go on," Russ says. The challenge of the road grips him, too.

On either side hillocks reach out into the salt flats. They rise into high ground to become a marching array of dunes, moving steadily southeastward, pushed by the driving wind that whips the surface grains from one shoulder to another and sends loose sand diving off the summits to drop and pile up on the valley floor, moving the sand mountains ceaselessly forward to encroach on roads and oases alike.

Streams of sand flow across the oiled road. "How come it got worse?" Cyndy says.

"Just appears that way," Russ says. "There's no loose sand in the *sabkhah* to get blown about."

A tall post with a broad cross marker bears a large "30" on its front side. Not much—just a kilo post. But it indicates that others have passed this way, ARAMCO engineers during construction of the road.

Top left: The great camel that blocks the road, defies the Rover's demand to get out of the way.

Bottom left: The *shamal* defies my attempt at a photo, for not even the earth can hold steady against its violence.

Below: A man and a boy emerge out of the dust, like coagulated masses of sand.

"There it is!" Cyndy cries. "Our big dune!"

Ash Sheikh wears a whirling robe of sand, its summit barely visible above distorted shoulders that seem to have taken to the air. In spite of the heavy wind, we continue. At kilo 80, an immense quiet descends, like the aftermath of a heavy snow. To the north the horizon blackens. The sky leans on the earth, building pressure to disgorge its bloat of swirling sand and air. Daylight diffuses through a dense filter of dust.

Russ brings the car to a stop and peers through the powder pouring like water down the windshield. A lone drift of sand from a nearby dune obstructs the road. Just behind it rears the dark bulk of an enormous camel. The sand is easily crossed, but the camel—legs spread wide on the blacktop—defies the Rover's demand to move out of the way. Gradually a herd emerges out of the murky dust: coagulated masses of sand. A small donkey bobs among the camels, carrying two riders—a man and a boy. Their faces are hidden behind the close wrap of their *ghutrah*. Russ braces to hold the door open, as he gets out. The remnant gusts tear at his hair and clothes.

"Where are you going?" I ask.

"To intercept these men."

Inside the car, the windows rattle, as waves of pressure burst against the metal body. It is as unyielding as the ugly barrier that swings its head toward me through the windshield. Russ raps on the window, and I roll it down. Scattering sand snags my mouth and eyes.

"The man wants you to ride the camels!" he shouts.

What's the matter with Russ? He can't be serious!

"A worse blow's coming," he says. "We're invited to wait it out in their tent."

The Bedouins, slow motioned by the thickness of the air, wrap *ghutrah* closer about their faces. These layers of fine cloth filter the breath and protect the eyes. The Bedu know their desert—we are inexperienced. Fear, born of caution, rises. Yet, security comes from a belief that to understand the Bedouin he must first be trusted.

"You're not taking this car off the road without Dee?"

Russ laughs. "How about camels? The man says their *bait* is not far."

How far is "not far" to the Bedouin, who is always on the move? The boy's long-barrelled rifle prods the baulking camel across the road. Slowly, the herd follows. The girls and I get out into a kind of no-man's-land, for the spectacular achievement of contemporary man to discover, to produce and to perfect tools for a better life is here rejected in favor of a camel and a goathair tent! We watch Russ discard this wonder of the twentieth century, as he drives the car onto firm ground off the road and locks it.

How swift and fluid a hot-blooded desert mare, but to get aboard the hulk of a camel is to suffer an opposing agony of beast and man. With beating, kicks and invectives the herders force a protesting female to the ground. Rumbling complaints belch loudly, and frothing saliva streams on the wind's ferocity. How fleet the jump of a Bedouin woman to the neck of a camel, as she leads a caravan from a well! But I am none of this—merely a conditioned response to an unopinionated assemblage of gears, bars and cushioned seats. I barely manage one leg over the hump, when violent rocking and lurching throw me head foremost across the back. I grasp the strap around the breastbone. No saddle, only a thin pad hanging precariously on the tail. My vertebrae strain, caught in the vice of a backward-forward thrust, as the camel rises and moves ahead.

"Hook your leg over the hump!" Russ shouts, his voice echoing through some turbulent separation.

This locomotion must be as distressing for the beast as for the rider, its long legs and neck achieving movement with a racking convulsion of effort. Now I appreciate the fortitude of a Bedouin woman, preferring to walk the sands than to suffer the merciless gait of a disgruntled camel! Antagonist of the Bedouin, this beast, whose supercilious smile declaims he alone will survive the final ravages of the desert.

The hairs of the back are knotted about bits of brush and pebbles that abrade my skin, for I do not wear the long garment of the nomad that protects him from his desert. I do not know where we are going, nor how to steer this conveyance, but I hang on. No rider am I, for there is neither rein nor halter with which to express control. Guest of the King I may be, now reduced to a despised and unwanted load!

The suffocating dust whirls on and on. "Not far . . ." the Bedouin said. From the back of a camel

Ropes squeak and the heavy
worsted rolls, as the wind
buffets the *bait ash sha'ar*.

in the fury of a *shamal*, time and distance are
measured by one's ability to endure. Through slits
of eyes, I watch the dust settle on a fuzz of curling
hair between little cat ears. The bobbing head and
neck detached from the island body in a sea of sand.
Do not stray, little head, for you alone lead this
mound to which I cling.

How much farther? When do we stop . . . ?

Existence blends into a misery of motion, as the
camels follow the swell of the desert. I have become
aching muscles, dry nostrils, watering and stinging
eyes. The whine of the wind becomes the cry of
children: "Ya Baahah must grow stronger than the
sun and the wind and the sand—stronger than
hunger and thirst . . ." But Abdullah is not here. He
has moved on with his family and the goats. The
head with the little cat ears bobs on, following the
one ahead—the one ahead . . .

The voices are shouts—real shouts! Between
finger slits I see small figures running, as they hasten
to catch up with the herd. And beyond—*bait ash
sha'ar*! The herd straggles behind. We who ride
are halted by the rush of children, who cry out in
tones that bring the camels to their knees without

protest. The hateful load is soon to be removed.

Legs in reverse repetition of rising, the solid bulk
hits the ground with a thump. A small girl in a thin
green dress throws herself across the neck of my
mount to hold it from rising. Her pliant body
wriggles forward, slim brown arm waving me to
dismount. Ankles locked together to hold me on the
back are not so quickly returned to life. Squirming
on the waving neck, the Bedouin child raises her
head. Through tangled strings of hair, her dark eyes
stare, startled by my uncovered face, my unusual
clothing—my difference from herself. Slipping off
the neck, she speeds away and darts under a tent:
first warning to those within.

I stumble as I walk, dazed muscles arousing to
normalcy. The wind pushes against my back, and I
am grateful for its aid. I hear the roll of heavy
worsted, as the roofs strain on the ropes, and the
closed walls surge in waves. The ropes, too, are
alive. Their knots squeak and tighten against pegs
that hold them to the roofs. Dried out fibers pull taut
against the ends wrapped about rock and buried in
the ground. Sand pelts the cloth and digs into the
weave. Pools of grains settle in the folds and dips,
coating the tents with an eerie resemblance to the

Ali bin Khalid sits within the
tent, watching dust patterns
in the blowing sand.

atmosphere, as though they, too, like the floating
men and the camels, emerged out of the dust.

Wrapped in this swirling *abayah* of gold, we no
longer know who or what we are.

Cyndy runs up and pulls on my arm. "Come on,"
she says. "These guys are going to give you coffee!"

Several men stand with Russ, feet anchored
against whipping *thaub*. Their gestures express
hospitality and welcome.

"*As salaam alaikum. Ahlan wa sahlan.* Come in out
of the storm." No questions asked. Nothing
demanded in return. A safeguard for him who roams
the waste. One day his needs may be as mine.

Russ' voice gains my attention. "Mansur bin
Abdullah waits for us."

I step around heaps of household goods that
strew the area: rolled bundles of tenting, scattered
poles, mounds of rope, boxes and saddlebags—
furnishings of another *bait*, its building interrupted
by the storm.

The Bedouins stand before a small white tent,
now visible between the black ones. Its flap is
thrown open, and the diffused daylight transmits a
warm glow through the bright orange print of the
lining. A pile of footwear builds at the opening, as
one by one the men step from heavy leather sandals
and disappear inside. I hesitate.

"It's all right," Russ says. "We're invited."

"But—all those men," I say. "I feel so awful!"
Wind blown—sand beaten—there's nothing I can
do to improve my appearance.

"We're in for a bit of luck," Russ says. "A
celebration in honor of the *sheikh's* son."

That settles it! "I'm not going in!" I say.

"Give them a chance," Russ says. "Khalid, the
son, brought his bride to the encampment last
night."

I unfasten the straps of my jodphur boots. The
girls do likewise. Wasn't it I who wanted to
introduce them to the real Arabia of the desert?
Our boots top the pile of sandals. I crouch to follow
Russ inside. A gust lashes at the nearby worsted
wall. I look up to see the blurred figure of a woman,
her dark eyes peering at me through a quivering
mask, above the rolling curtain of the *bait ash sha'ar*.

Within the tent, the Bedouins sit in council, in the
sight of Allah none more elevated than the other.
Thus have the elders always gathered in the

Sheikh's *majlis* to adjudicate, arbitrate and defend
the individual, the family, the tribe, on the plains
of the Summan, in the sands of the Rub' al Khali,
along the fertile Wadi al Miyah. Feet, thick skinned
and calloused are concealed under robes. Nimble
fingers polish amber prayer beads, as they count off
the ninety-nine names of Him who is the final judge.

The word of the *ulema* is law: "Oh, daughter of
Aneyza, return to your father, for your bad temper
weakens your husband's tent." "Seek revenge on
the Al Awazim who have stolen our camels."

Not ascetic, these faces that live with God, but
rugged, proud, strong, like the jut of a *jabal* out of
flatness. Pride has carved the firm lip of courage, the
unflinching stance of honor.

On a mattress behind the tentpole the girls and I
sit apart, alongside, but not within the circle of men.
Our presence and dress flaunt the codes of the
group, and I feel the pressure of being a woman.
The hum of relaxed voices around me seems to carry
over the pronouncements of ages: "You daughters
of men, destroy not the greatness of what we are";
"Purity is long lived, in the isolation of the desert, in
the confines of the *hareem* . . ." The *hareem*—
Muslim family women and their sacred place. No,
we are not as they, nor do we belong in this circle
of men.

Today the men have not come to judge, but to
celebrate. They smile and chat, questioning Russ on
desert movements he has observed, on the visit to
Riyadh of the Governor of the Eastern Province.

A little boy sits apart, staring through the open
flap at the flying sand outside. Perhaps he seeks one
who has not entered yet. What would he say, if I
offered him green parks and playgrounds, a bicycle,
plenty of food, and books with which to learn and
to grow? I read the answer in his intent young face:
"The Glorious Koran is my teacher. In it I am fed
and clothed. How easily folded and moved are the
black walls of my *bait ash sha'ar*. The winds of the
desert tell me of strength and the courage of
warriors . . ." He has more than I—security of self—
this child, who watches dust patterns in the blowing
sand.

Unruffled by the fury of nature, an old man slips
inside the tent and stands as in a vacuum, eyes
seeking a focus. Translucent hands clutch the neck
of his gold trimmed cloak. A lingerer from other
days, he has come to sit within the circle.

The child jumps up. "Take me, Uncle!" He tugs

The old uncle takes his place
in the circle, and Ali climbs
onto his lap.

at the old man's robe.

The newcomer sits with the group, spreads his knees, and sets the boy on his lap. A murmur of mirth accompanies each kinsman's greeting, offered in response to the elder's eyes that study them all. A place was made for the old man on the far side of the circle beyond the tentpole. The center pole of the *bait ash sha'ar* signifies the seat of honor. But this glaring canvas cover is not honored by the shades of former tribesmen, the salt stains of distant deserts, the wind's stretch of warp and woof. It is without meaning.

"Who is he?" Linda asks. I do not know, but I am alert to uneasiness.

Without warning, tranquility shatters. An outburst of violence contorts the old man's face. He jumps up with what agility he can, tumbling the boy to the ground. A dish of dates overturns against the force of an aimless foot. With one long stride he advances into the circle and thrusts an accusing finger at me.

"*Imsh*! *Imsh*! *Hareem*—out!" These words of anger are telling us to leave.

I shudder in alarm. Were we not invited? Given the most comfortable seat—the bridal couch, I am discomfited beyond words. Tense, the girls look to me.

The circle is not disturbed. The faces wear masks of politeness and amusement. I meet the old man's stare head on, without animosity, for I know his reaction to females in the *majlis* is correct for him. But I wince, as he cries again: "Out—*hareem*!".

Hands hold the irate tribesman.

Cyndy says, "I don't want to stay. Let's go."

The circle presses against the side wall of the tent. We would have to push by, stumble over boots, and our leaving would acknowledge a fault—we should not be here.

Then, laughter ripples through the circle of faces. "Ho, Uncle! Since when have you been afraid of the *hareem*?"

And, a second voice, calm, authoritative. "Good Uncle, we have guests . . ."

A young man stands just inside the flap. He wears a dark blue *thaub*, finely tailored, his red and white *ghutrah* thrown casually across his shoulder. He steps through the circle of men and rests a hand on the elder's arm.

"Today we celebrate. Come, Uncle, sit with us . . ."

The old man stares blankly, as the newcomer

leads him back to his place.

"Hold me, Uncle! Hold me!" the small boy cries, once again clambering onto the old man's lap.

The newcomer addresses himself to Russ. "I am Khalid bin Mansur. You and your family honor my house by your presence." He assures us that his great uncle meant no harm. Age has made him *majnun*—detached from reality.

Order restored, the men embrace Khalid with affection and enthusiasm. Russ is introduced to them all: the father, brothers, cousins, uncles—all relatives, tribesmen. Then, Khalid bin Mansur takes the boy in his arms. "Sons are a man's riches," he says, kissing the child on each cheek. Setting him on the floor, he sends the boy on an errand outside the tent.

The storm's diffused light glows brilliant through the orange canvas. "I bought the tent in Kuwait," Khalid says, offering cigarettes from the deep pocket in his *thaub*. "One thousand *riyal*. Was it too much?"

"Nothing is too costly that provides comfort, protection—and pleasure." Russ leans forward to pass his lighter across the circle.

Khalid's brother jumps to his feet. "And such pleasure, *ya akhuiy*!" He touches Khalid's hands, kissing him on the face, the nose, the forehead. The rest of the men follow suit, kissing and embracing Khalid for a second round of congratulations. "May your life be blest. May Allah reward you with many sons and daughters."

Khalid returns the warmth of unrestrained family affection. Natural impulses, unscarred by the enforced stigma of unmanliness for a man to express emotion. Like Khalid, the desert does not forsake its majesty in moods of tenderness. The flowering of a dry stalk carries the same open declaration, as a man's pride in a son.

"Abu-Ali"—father of Ali, as the son is called "Ali bin Khalid", Ali, the son of Khalid. Family ties closely woven. The strength of unity—insurance for survival.

I read it all before me, for the *shamal* has made me an observer of the privacy of men. The white tent, *jihaaz*, was part of the marriage contract along with clothes and money. This party for men alone, a tradition the great uncle could not ignore.

Khalid bin Mansur is a departure from the usual Bedouin. His roots are in the desert, but his clothes, his step into commercialism belong to another

Khalid bin Mansur pours
desert coffee from a brass pot
into small handleless cups.

The tribesmen sit in a circle
within the tent, conversing
and fingering prayer beads.

world. He owns a business in Kuwait importing
Sony products. Khalid comes to the desert for the
regeneration of his spirit, and here his sons will grow
up, steeped in the traditions of the Bedouin.

Ali bin Khalid returns, holding a brass cylinder in
both hands. He seeks between the long robes for a
path to reach his father. An older boy follows,
carrying a wide-beaked brass coffee pot that steams
under its tall lid.

"*Tafaddalu,*" Khalid says. "*Qahwah!*" (coffee).

The circle reforms. Only Russ has remained in
his place. Khalid takes the coffee pot, adjusting the
scraps of cloth that serve as a hot pad for the handle.
Instantly, Ali pours a column of tiny porcelain cups
from the cylinder and offers it to his father. Khalid
nestles the cups in his right hand, balanced between
thumb and forefinger. In one graceful movement he
starts the amber liquid flowing into the first cup,
sweeps the pot upwards, then down to the cup's rim
without spilling a drop. The flow of the brew, the
aroma of the spices, the anticipation of taste
tantalize we who wait.

The first cup is offered to me, then to Linda,

Cyndy and Russ. Khalid waits and watches as we
take the first sip. The coffee is light, hot and fragrant
with cardamom—a taste to be acquired. Three sips
the cup holds—no more. Again the coffee flows. No
one else has been served. Khalid extends the pot for
a third round.

"*La, shukran*—no, thank you," I say. The cup
returns filled.

Cyndy is in distress. She doesn't like coffee and
cardamom makes it worse. Her cup will not stay in
Khalid's hand. It keeps coming back full! She
watches as her father's cup is rinsed in a bowl of
water, filled with coffee and served to the next man
in the circle.

"Dad!" Cyndy cries to her father's back. "How
do you turn it off?"

"Just shake the cup with your wrist." Cyndy
does—it works—and she grins.

Each man in turn accepts the coffee three times,
until all have been served. Only then does Khalid
bin Mansur enjoy the brew.

The broad beaked brass pot, *dallah*, repository of
hospitality and luxury, is drained of coffee. The first

"Poor little things," Linda says, as she hurries to help the baby animals against the storm.

Detail of the embroidered *qata* with rifle hanging on a tentpole.

round only has been served. Palates are barely warmed, inquiries concerning family members scattered throughout the *dirrah* scarcely begun. Happiness in reassociation with Khalid must be reiterated again and again. The afternoon will be long.

I shift uncomfortably on the mattress. Cyndy's eyes turn from the printed pattern of the walls to the older boy, who takes the pot for a refill. "How much longer?" she says.

Linda twists to uncurl her legs. Our skirts will not allow the relaxed position of the Bedouins. Khalid speaks to Ali. The young son leans from his father's lap and reaches the dish of dates. Plump fingers retrieve the strays spilt by the uncle's foot onto the sandy rug. He comes outside the circle of men and pauses by the tentpole. His white *thaub* is brushed with sand dust; his gold-stitched *kufiyah* (cap) snug on his child's head. He stands in front of me offering the dish.

My hygienic upbringing is outweighed by the traditions of Bedouin hospitality. The round, dark eyes hold mine. There is no question of refusal. Ali offers the best his father has. Such a serious young face—without fear or question of who we are. My fingers touch the sticky mass, the sprinkles of sand, the clinging black hairs from being stored in a goatskin.

Cyndy sees the dish coming. "Can't we go—now!"

Again I judge the distance between the men and the tent wall. Perhaps we could just squeeze past. But the opening is not ours to use, for an arm in a blue flowered sleeve and wearing gold bangles extends a coffee pot to Khalid. Then, it withdraws.

The women and girls, the tousle-headed child in the thin green dress, the eyes that watched above the curtain of the *bait ash sha'ar*: I must find them. I lean toward Russ.

"The girls and I are going out."

"You can't!"

"We're tired of sitting. We'll visit the *hareem*."

Khalid is serving more coffee, as Russ continues. "You can't just walk into those tents!"

"Then, ask Khalid."

Khalid pauses in his task. "You wish something?"

Russ ponders an appropriate answer. It does not belong to the desert, but rather to our house in Ras Tanura, the brownstones of New York, the condominiums of California. "My wife wishes to

pay her respects to your wife."

The words hang above the circle of men. They float from *ghutrah* to *ghutrah*, gather volume in the dead silence, provoke a sudden freeze of amber beads, drain the warmth from golden walls, shout into every ear.

I shudder, not knowing what to expect from the indignant eyes, nor will I surrender to the scoffs of what I do not understand. Khalid eases the moment. He speaks directly to Russ—the polite, expansive host.

"Yes, of course. The houses of hair. Certainly our guests are welcome there."

I search for shoes half buried in the heap of sandals and piled sand, and do not stop to put them on. We step into the wind, the girls and I, just as Ali rushes past us and ducks into a black tent.

"You must come back for tea," Khalid calls after me, but I have no intention of entering that nuptial

Family possessions have been hastily piled against the dividing curtain in the *mahram* —and on the sandy floor an infant lies asleep.

Linda and Cyndy approach the *majlis* where embroidered curtains have been extended to create an entranceway.

tent again.

The *shamal* snares us with reduced intensity. Hair whips my face. Cyndy tucks her long strands under her jacket and fastens the buttons. We start to put on our shoes.

"Oh!" Cyndy cries, pressing into the wind to reach a huddle of goats against a clump of brush. Their long white ears are being blown straight up.

"Poor little things," Linda says. "They can't see." She brushes encrusted sand from their eyes. A faint bleating spurs further concern. "Can't we put them somewhere?"

"They're all right," I say. "They belong here." It doesn't help. "You have sand on your face," I add.

"I can brush it off. They can't..."

We walk to the nearest *bait ash sha'ar*. Its tightly woven walls hold back the wind. The ropes quiver, as the roof rolls with the gusts, and the loose fringe flaps ominously. I peer over the worsted wall. A curtain of heavy, white wool, the *qata*, beautifully embroidered in blazing red and black, divides the

tent into two rooms. The larger one is closed in. The extended *qata* in front of the second is tied to support ropes, allowing for additional space and creating an entranceway. Now, there is no sign of anyone. We step over the ropes and enter the traditional *majlis*.

A feeling of permanence pervades. Tomorrow the room may be torn down, its parts lashed to the backs of camels, to be reassembled elsewhere, but the room will be the same: a well-worn rug spread on the floor, a camel saddle padded with a red quilt and topped with a black sheepskin, a rifle in a leather case with colorful bandolier hanging from hooks on the center pole together with a handsome brown *bisht* (cloak) trimmed with gold braid. And the coffee fire—its pots and tools ready for use.

"Why didn't we come in here?" Linda asks. "The coals are still hot."

"I'm sure Khalid wanted to show off the nuptial tent," I say.

"That's where his bride lives," Linda says in answer to Cyndy's questioning look.

Broad beaked brass coffee pots stand ready for use, alongside an incense burner, mortar and pestle, brass cylinder containing the cups, and a dish of dates.

The girl holds us with her gaze—"Do not go," the eyes plead. She is *arousa*—the bride of Khalid bin Mansur.

Four brass coffee pots stand about a shallow hole scooped from the sand in which cakes of dung still glow. The coffee must have been made here. The long, black bean roaster and rake lie on the sand, and near them a wooden dish for cooling the beans. A brass mortar and pestle await the roasted beans for pulverizing. An incense burner, trimmed with mirror chips, and a plate of dates ready for use.

The making and serving of coffee is the exclusive province of the men. Certainly, Khalid hadn't made it for us. Then—who? No one is about, only the wind rolling the heavy roof, and a goat mournfully bleating. We step around the artifacts and turn to leave.

The embroidered *qata* moves, as hennaed hands, dark against the white wool, push down upon the curtain. Above the hands peers the impish face of a little girl. Her tight curly hair, more tangled than my own, swirls against the shoulders of her green dress. For the second time our eyes meet, not across the neck of a camel, but above the coffee pots. Then she is gone.

The glance over the *qata* is a purpose served: the

child sent by a woman to attract our attention. I responded once before along the Darb al Kunhuri with disastrous results. Dare I try again? We approach the *mahram*. Its face is partly open. A broad striped curtain lies on the ground. Someone unhooked it from the roof. Someone wanted us here.

Piles of baggage clutter the dim interior, as though hastily deposited—the household belongings of a family all dumped into the womens' quarters. The occupants must have recently arrived and hurried off to other tasks before setting the room in order. The *majlis* must be readied first for the comfort of the men and the welcoming of guests.

How much may be learned of a family from its possessions. The disarray on the sandy floor displays the basic needs of nomad life. Every article to be picked up and moved, as the tribe follows the course of fodder and water. But, new saddlebags, a velvet prayer rug, a full bolt of cloth, tent strips that have never faced the wind tell another story. Someone new to the desert has arrived: the bride of Khalid bin Mansur.

I stare through the shadows seeking her. Against the back wall loom the high hoops of the *maksar*. On the ground are strewn pots and pans, a small metal trunk with painted flowers, sacks of staples, and dung cakes.

Linda is suddenly excited. "Look! A baby!"

On the ground in front of the prayer rug and wrapped in a grey cloth like a bundle of provisions, an infant lies asleep. The storm has laid its own light blanket of sand on the child. Linda bends forward for a closer look.

"Stay away from the child," I warn. "Somebody must be near."

The veiled outline of a woman, reticent as the shadows, rises from behind the *maksar*. She drifts forward, hesitant to cross the open area along the rear of the tent.

I greet her. "God's peace upon you . . ."—poetry of speech torn from its roots by my foreignness. Like a startled bird, she wings to the wall, blending into the blackness.

"*Masaa' al khair*." (Goodness attend you this afternoon). The continued greeting does not move her. I bend over the infant. "The baby—is it yours?"

The woman starts toward the heaped bundles where the child sleeps, then hesitates, not knowing what to do. Her eyes glisten through the mask—young eyes, rimmed with *kohl* (black eye lining) to

The wind fights with a woman
to gain possession of her veils.

enhance their size and beauty. A black veil covers
her head and shoulders, and her light blue dress is
printed with flowers of deep cornflower blue. Her
hands, pressed to the mask, are soft, unmarked by
the toil of building a *bait*, scrubbing pots with sand,
sewing coarse homespun with rough thread so that
the fingers bleed.

This is Khalid's bride—the *arousa*. Now, the same
eyes that watched us enter the bridal tent stare at
me with frightened uncertainty.

Sensitive to the vibrations of others, Linda turns
away. "She doesn't want us here."

We are a threat to what must be: the complete
seclusion of a bride—her need to protect the infant.

We retreat beyond the dropped curtain. The wind
finds us. The girl hurries forward, her gesture a
plea: you may not stay—but, do not go! Is it
curiosity, a sense of kinship with Linda—a girl like
herself—that emboldens her? Or, has she renounced
guests—a fault in any tent—she, who may not
communicate with anyone. Clearly, we present a
problem.

Linda tugs at my arm to leave. The tinkle of bells
beneath the veil bids us stay. Deliberately, the girl
squats near the tent face, her gaze holding us. The
sound of the bells says what her voice will not: do
not go.

Tentatively, we enter conversation. She
acknowledges with a nod that Kuwait City is her
home. By her marriage she aligns her merchant
family with a prestigious tribe. The story is not new.

"She doesn't seem very happy," Linda says,
perhaps recalling the joyous wedding of her cousin.

Personal happiness must be acquired. To bring
honor to the family is the important thing—*her*

family, to which a woman always belongs, for in
marriage she retains her own name. How alone she
must feel, sent to the desert through an arranged
union with no voice in her future, and not even
present when the contract was signed. The family
women would have bathed, depilated, scented and
exquisitely gowned her for delivery to the
bridegroom's house. Festivities of feasting and
dancing went on without her, there in the bright
lights of Kuwait City. The joy is for guests. Affairs of
the family are private. The celebrations are not for
her—the bride—the *arousa*.

A long chain with keys dangles from her hair and
rests on her lap. The keys to a small metal box
containing personal treasures—the right of every
Bedouin woman to own one.

What future awaits this lonely bride married to
the desert, to the stringent laws of the tents? The
qualities of self-confidence, assertiveness and
responsibility of choice I might encourage in Linda
may not be offered to this girl. She must be content
with marriage and the family bond.

Support ropes intertwine like a cat's cradle across
a narrow corridor between two *bait ash sha'ar*.
The wind whips between them in its unbroken
sweep across the wastes. A black form emerges
through the *shamal*—a woman carrying a bundle of
arfaj on her head. The wind fights to gain possession
of her veils, as she drops the firewood alongside the
overhang and takes refuge under the roof. We alone
remain exposed to the storm. Ill-clothed, a sorry
sight to women of the desert. I draw the girls close
for mutual protection.

Something other than wind tugs at my skirt.
Eyes blinded by the sting of sand, I follow the pull to
the second tent, its curtain dropped. My vision clears
sufficiently to catch sight of a green dress diving
behind a woman's skirts. "*Tafaddali . . .*" an assuring
voice repeats. "Come in."

A tall woman urges me to sit, and taking their
hands, brings the girls under the protection of the
roof. The mother moves about, and the child of the
green dress has difficulty in keeping behind her
parent's red one. Laughing, the woman tries to free
herself from clutching hands.

"*Bintik?*" she asks, beckoning Cyndy. "Your
daughter?" Cyndy holds back. "*Wafa!*" the mother
calls. "*Shuf*—look at this new friend."

But Wafa will not expose so much as a ragged

hair. She has performed the ultimate in bringing us here.

"She is shy, my young one."

"But fast as the gazelle," I say, remembering the green dress slithering from the camel.

Wafa twists her lithe body for a quick look at Cyndy, then hides behind the *maksar*. Cyndy is barely more sociable, still dazed from the wind. The woman's eyes smile through the mask. We are a family—they are a family. We are in need of what she can give: refuge and comfort. There is no strangeness in need between families.

A child's cry fills the tent. Wafa rushes to a crib of woven palm spines. She tries to reach into it, but the sides are too tall. She jumps up and down and yells. The mother lifts an infant from the crude bed. She squats and hugs the baby, smoothing its faded blue dress, adjusting its gold trimmed bonnet. Wafa sneaks closer to hide behind her mother.

Scarred and work-worn hands toss the baby into the air. Its laughter gurgles above the wind, like drops of water splashing into a well. The mother holds the infant close, and the mask intercepts her kiss on its cheek.

In this moment of cultural confrontation, the squeaking strain of cloth and rope becomes the bellowing of camel calf and bleating of lamb, as, with the return of herds from grazing, they race toward their mothers to be nudged and licked. The human child must wait for that moment of privacy to savor the touch of a mother's lips against its cheek. Cyndy moves close to me, and I put my arm around her. You see—love is not less because of a piece of black cloth.

I tell the girls we should leave, but the Bedouin mother stops me. She tucks the infant under her arm and heads for the rear of the tent. The keys on the end of her long chain clink together as she moves. Stooping, she drags forward her small metal box standing against the *ruwaaq* (side curtain). Scraped and dented, its yellow and pink flowers bloom gaudily in the shadows. Her eager hands, stained by years of application of henna, pull up the chain anchored under her head veil and find the key. She unlocks the box, pushing back the lid to rest on its hinges. I watch her dig through a jumble of treasures: a roll of lace, a dress length of purple and silver cloth, a cracked mirror, a bottle of *kohl*, a paper sack of incense. Her hand uncovers a packet of candy.

Again she squats close to me, the infant nestled on her lap, and pulls at the paper to open the roll of candy. The small boy from Khalid's *majlis*, Ali bin Khalid, runs in. He is quick to grab the candy. Several bright pieces fall on the sand. The mother retrieves the packet and offers it to Cyndy.

"I don't want any," she says.

"Take one," I urge. "She is offering the best she has."

Two drops of red color the center of Cyndy's palm. She forces a smile. Linda takes her piece, and the mother gives the packet to Ali.

"Your son?" I ask.

"*Na'am*. Yes." Her voice glows. "*Waladi*—my son!"

Three baby goats sleep near the crib. Their necks are held by loops of wool tied to a length of rope pegged into the ground. This tent is a home, where love reaches out to all who enter. Its furnishings are sparse and well used: mended curtains, bedding neatly folded, blackened pots and kettles stacked around a hearth of stones. The woman's deep red dress—a color favored by so many Ajman women— is stained and faded.

Not so her spirit. Life is a treasure to be nurtured and guarded, not undermined by destructive emotions. Today, her children are more meaningful than yesterday, now that Khalid bin Mansur, her husband, has taken a second wife.

Two older boys join the family. They have served today's apprenticeship in the *majlis* and return home, as any child from school.

"I am Umm Nawaf," the woman says, touching the shoulder of the oldest boy, for the mother is known by the name of her first son. Mother of Nawaf.

She asks if I have sons, and I tell her—no. "*Bintain*—two daughters only. I am Umm Linda, and the younger one is Cyndy."

"*Inshallah*, you shall have sons."

Her blessing is a fervent Arab wish. Spontaneously, she bends forward and offers her baby for my lap, another boy, Mohammed. For this moment she shares with me the joy of holding a son.

The mask covering her face also conceals her feelings. What is it like to be a wife whose husband enjoys a new bride? I cannot answer. My security has never been invaded. Here, it is the custom, sanctioned by the Prophet: "Take unto yourself two—or three—or four wives. But treat them all alike—make of them equals."

The mother of Khalid's sons
embraces the youngest—
another boy, Mohammed.

This home is Umm Nawaf's, hers and her children's. Here Khalid will spend equal nights. Here he will bring a dress for a dress—a ring for a ring—food in equal shares. The task of survival goes on uninterrupted by a woman's feelings. However inexperienced in desert life, the new bride will be another pair of hands to lighten the load of the women's lot.

"Does your husband have two wives?"

"No," I say. How can I expect her to appreciate the pleasure of a man and a woman sharing independence and accomplishment?

She directs her gaze toward the other *bait ash sha'ar*, which she knows I have visited. "She is Khalid's new wife," she confirms. Her tone is sure, unemotional, revealing a fact. The lift of her head reminds she is Umm Nawaf, mother of sons. There is no greater name.

A commotion and loud voices startle. Umm Nawaf jumps up and I follow.

Women and girls—flying bobs of black—bustle about a high red truck. Two women stand on the truck bed, tossing out tent strips, poles, waterskins and sacks of household goods. Baby goats join the melée. They jump from the truck onto the growing pile of furnishings, there to be chased off and cornered by shouting children. Women drag boxes and loaded saddlebags alongside the last tent, while others seek shelter under its roof.

"*Yalla*! (let's go)," Umm Nawaf cries. Infant in arms, green dress dragging behind, she hurries off to help her relatives with the unloading. How often have they done this—while their men sip coffee in the *majlis*?

How many pairs of hands have grown old wrestling with the heavy worsted walls? How many children have learned the meaning of survival, as they helped their mothers drag the strips of goathair into position for raising—wind or rain, heat or flood? The building and re-building of the *bait ash sha'ar* goes on without end.

Today there is the truck. Gift of technology. Is it easier to lift great loads to a high truck bed, than to couch a camel? Mechanical parts must succumb to the desert's unpreparedness to keep them moving. To travel by truck is to be confined to areas close to supplies of gasoline. The automobile turned us into a nation of nomads. Conversely, it may serve to settle the Bedu.

Above the chattering within the tent, a strident voice shouts for water. A girl in a skirt of cornflower blue slips outside to where goatskins of water lie on air-cooled beds of *arfaj*. She unwinds the rope from the neck of a goatskin, pours water in a bowl, and reties the neck. A glance toward us, as she hurries past and hands the bowl to a large and domineering woman. The matriarch raises her mask and drinks, passing the bowl to her companions.

Again an order to the bride. Against the strong wind, the younger woman reaches for one of the tent ropes near the roof and pulls on it, but her hands drag the rough surface. The matriarch shouts a second order. Again the girl tugs on the rope, but it does not give. The wind disarrays her veil and mask. The blue skirt flutters helplessly, like a bird in pain.

Linda asks what she is doing, and I explain she is trying to tighten the ropes to take the slack out of the roof.

"How can she see anything?" Linda is upset. "Why doesn't somebody help her?" But no one does.

Impulsively, Linda hurries to her side. She places her hands on the rope next to the brightly hennaed

Umm Khalid, mother of
Khalid, holds her sister's child,
as she bargains with me for
Linda to become a second wife.

ones, and together they pull. The rope moves. The slip knot holds. The roof gives up its slack.

"That's hard work," Linda says, rubbing her palms along her skirt. She stares at her hands, reddened from the coarse hemp.

For a moment the bride stands there, uncertain. Then, real fear glistening in her eyes, she dashes behind the tent.

The matriarch has seen us. She peers out over the face of the *bait*. What does she think of me, this woman who directs the life of the camp? She steps out from under the roof, pulling her many veils securely about her rotund body.

I walk to meet her. Assertiveness may offset my shortcomings. "*As salaam alaikum,*" I say, holding down my flying hair. Her quick nod acknowledges. Powdery sand showers her bosom from the crinkles in her stiff calico mask. As from the depth of a tomb, the eyes direct a look that pierces, but glints of humor sparkle between fleshy lids that wrinkle behind the slits.

"Umm Khalid?" I say. Only the mother of Khalid, oldest son of the encampment's leader, would rule the *hareem* of his tents. Her nod is curt, for her

interest is not with me. She shouts another woman to her. A deep, throaty laugh shakes the ample body and rolls the string of colored beads beneath coarse veiling.

"*Bintik?*" she indicates Linda.

Something in her manner arouses discomfort. "Yes. My daughter."

"Very pretty—very strong." Her gaze records Linda's assets. My instincts are as sharp as hers. I send the girls packing, back to their father. Black eyes follow them, quick to observe Linda has remained nearby. The second woman speaks up. Her son will pay three sheep and one camel—maybe two camels—the finest *dhulul*.

"A generous price," Umm Khalid agrees. "We can arrange a marriage for your daughter."

I pretend not to understand. Why isn't Russ here with his flowery phrases instead of drinking coffee? Oh, the endless coffee! How does one decline without offending? My twentieth century phrases are no good here: "Oh—how lovely! Well, we must discuss it." Only one solution: leave now!

Umm Khalid urges. "You accept this generous price?"

103

A Bedouin woman twists wool into a thread on her spindle. The Muslim world holds her privacy inviolate.

I stumble over words. "She is too young—only a schoolgirl." What's the matter with me? I don't have to acknowledge anything! She does not belong to my life—this dominating black bosom!

"No! No—she is old enough! She will make a strong wife!" The words are black strings threatening Linda's freedom.

"It is impossible. No, thank you." What am I thanking her for? It's crazy! The wind has turned my senses.

"Wait! Look!" Umm Khalid shouts.

What power of her dominance draws me to look back? She holds a child in her arms, so handsome, so unusual. I stare in amazement, for it does not belong in the arms of the black one. The almond eyes are golden brown, the flesh tones pink, fluffy hair the color of sand. I raise the camera.

"Yes, you must!" Umm Khalid is delighted. "Take all the pictures you want," she says, artfully.

The child wears a dress of turquoise blue, printed with peacock feathers. About her neck dangle several heavy necklaces: amber beads, silver coins, a leather amulet to appease evil spirits. The small wrists and fingers jingle with bangles and rings. Umm Khalid raises the child in her arms, then points to Linda. She repeats her offer of marriage, shrewdly confirming such a lovely granddaughter could be mine, for the bride price is offered on behalf of the child's father.

The only escape is not to listen. I keep on taking pictures long after the film runs out. Unexpectedly, Umm Khalid returns the child to the tent, and I hear Khalid's voice behind me. "Mrs. Nicholson, you did not come back for tea . . ."

We join Russ outside the *jihaaz*, where he puts on his boots. "We must return to Ras Tanura," he tells Khalid.

"But—we have not killed a sheep for you," Khalid says.

"It is we who are at fault," Russ says. "You have shared with us the comforts of your home."

"May Allah protect you through the storm."

"May he enrich your family a thousandfold."

"You must come again. We will have a great feast."

"*Inshallah . . .*" Russ says.

"*Inshallah. . . .*" If it is the will of God.

I dread having to mount a camel in the face of all those women! And, *alhamdulillah* (God be praised) I do not have to. Khalid heads for a small car on the far side of the tent: a Volkswagen with four-wheel drive. "I will take you to the road," he says.

Several men, chanting in rhythm, lift the car and swing it around. We squeeze in. A flash of blue skirt disappears behind a black wall. The ride in the Volkswagen is worse than the Rover but better than the camels. The tough *arfaj* scrapes the undercarriage, as though it would tear through the flooring. The car tilts precariously over buried rock, but Khalid knows his desert. Soon the thin black ribbon of oiled road comes in sight, and with it, the Rover.

"*Fiamanillah*—goodbye."

"*Fiamanilkarim.*"

Thick, yellow dust filters down, as the wind blows itself out. Cyndy works at the picnic basket and finds a packet of fried chicken.

"By the way, Russ," I say, "Could you use a couple of camels?"

"I know what that woman was talking about," Linda protests. "And you don't have to repeat it!"

Russ unwraps a piece of chicken. "Guess I pulled a bad one, suggesting to Khalid that you call on his wife."

Linda is interested. "How come?"

"In the Arab world one must respect the privacy of the family. I was a stranger. It was not my place to speak of his wife."

"That's like pretending women don't exist!" Linda is fast learning to uphold the rights of women.

"Far from it," her father says, laughing. "Women are powerful in all societies. Just look at your mother!"

Touches of lavender reach into the valleys, as the invasion of dust lessens. The rippled slopes of the great dunes shoulder one against the other. Toneless utterances of the desert whisper through parched stalks, race up the shimmering gradients, and find voice in a golden plume whirling outwards off the crests. As we roll through the drifting dust, I sense I am no longer a mere observer, but have become a participant. Under the familiar lights of Ras Tanura, I know I have left something of myself within the worsted walls of the *bait ash sha'ar*.

PART V
The Wells of `Uwaynah (October 1963)

THE CAMEL
Like an ostrich pursued by night,
   driven by darkness,
Overwhelmed by fear from wind, lightning
   and thunder;
Like a meteor rushing to earth
Your camel, my messenger, dashed forward,
Allowing you no chance to be hailed.

Coming downhill it slithers sideways
Like a dragon, like a drunk.
All the same going up or
Down, over sand or rough land.

Its hooves throw stones everywhere like bullets
And are burning fire to the touch.
Its jump climbs to the clouds,
And its neck slopes like a valley.

In a display of beauty, strength, and grace,
Your velvet-coated thoroughbred
Is unyielding like iron—
Agile like a gazelle.

July—August—September. The summer months of 1963 find the desert afire. Scorching heat turns sand and rock into ovens, shrivels dry brush, dries up sources of water. Camel herds huddle together, ragged humps emaciated. They wait for the stirring of a lone herder who searches dawn's horizon. He has watched each dawn since the first day of Jumada II—the month of the Muslim calendar that in 1963 falls in the month of September. On this, the thirteenth day the camels lift their heads, for the man shouts with joy.

"Oh, you suffering daughters of the desert! Great is the goodness of Allah! She has come—Suhail!—lighting this dawn with her promise. Soon our tribesmen shall return to the land!"

The *sheikh*, too, sees the morning star from quarters on the edge of the village where the tribe has camped throughout summer's devastation. Suhail—Canopus—has come with its promise of release from confinement, stifling heat, and the wet Kaus wind from the south.

But the terrible, wet heat continues throughout Jumada II. Then, in October, a new voice rings across the land. Roll after roll of thunder reverberate around the sky. First rains plummet to earth in streamers of black strings from the freed masks of thunderheads.

"Come, my children! Pull up the stakes! Let fall the poles! Drop the roof! We go to meet the new grasses of the rain!"

In Ras Tanura the rain spatters the roof and garden. "Pack the food! Throw in the sleeping bags! Rout out Dee! For we are heading for the desert!"

The golden glory of Ash Sheikh welcomes us back after the long summer's absence. His cloak shimmers in the morning sun—brocaded patterns

Twisted limbs of the *athl* tree have witnessed life's defiance of the desert, time and history.

The solitary *athl* tree at Al
Hinnah. Its broad canopy of
leaves harbors the secret of
the town's desertion by the
Bani Khalid.

of wet sand. At Kilo 100 on the Northern Access
Road we turn off to Fadhili. Russ locks the front
wheels into four-wheel drive. We speed across the
sabkhah, churn up the hill of soft sand imprinted
with rain, then slow and return to check the safe
crossing of the red truck.

Our desert skills have improved. Fear of the
unknown has become joy of discovery, confidence
in self reliance, love of the open land, a kinship with
those we seek. Up and over. Up and over. Endless
kilometers of *dikakah* country. "Look! There are
tents—and camel riders!" Eyes to the thunderheads,
we beat the downpour to the timeless *athl* tree of
Al Hinnah.

Suddenly, we come on mud brick walls—
crumbling, roofless, abandoned. Forgotten homes
now playgrounds for burrowing beetles and long-
legged spiders. All is deserted, even the deep wells
with tall rock casements where buckets were hung
and lowered. One well remains potable, and here

wandering Bedu bring camel herds to water.

Many stories relate the abandonment of Al
Hinnah—and Thaj, nine kilometers south,
metropolis for converging caravans long before
Islam. Drought? Disease? Or, was it Ibn Saud, who
enforced a change of *dirrah* during his conquest of
Al Hasa? The Bani Khalid rightful tribe of the *dirrah*
were replaced by the Awazim, who eventually
returned to the north. The Bani Khalid never
reclaimed their settlements. So, Al Hinnah, like a
disgraced virgin daughter, died under the dishonor
of occupation by a lesser tribe. The desert law of
purity—even as a purebred mare, tainted by a
degraded foal, becomes unworthy to uphold the
honor of her breed.

What is left is the driven sand, turbulent winds,
and indications of defiant life: animal droppings,
bright emerald blades of new grass, a fragile yellow
flower, stones marking a child's grave. And the *athl*
tree, landmark of place and history, whose canopy

Herdsmen chant, as they toss
leather buckets into the deep
well and bring up water to be
poured into the *haudh*.

of leaves resounds with the forgotten shouts of
children, barking of dogs, laughter of women,
squeak of ropes on the wells, whinny of a mare, and
the muted voice of prayer. On this night we build
our *bait* beneath the great tree.

Early morning brings camel herds filling the
emptiness of Al Hinnah. Youngsters run alongside
their mothers; pack animals carry large troughs and
buckets. Each group keeps within itself and awaits
its turn at the well.

"*Ya* Jannon! *Ya* Lataan! *La*, Habaab, no!" She
shrills a little tune, the child in the rose print dress,
who calls the camels by name. Her bamboo stick
lands a stinging lash against a truant calf, as she
darts among the forest of legs. A younger brother
jumps and grabs a dangling lead rope from a long
neck. One flick of a hoof, and the beast could knock
the boy over, but it doesn't. It halts as though
anchored to the thick trunk of the *athl* tree.

Boys single out a beast and drive it forward to be
couched and laden with skins of water for some
distant encampment. A herdsman jumps atop a
high back to loosen the *haudh* (trough) and drop it
to the ground, while others toss down buckets and
ropes. In these troughs of pomegranate wood and
leather the animals are watered: tall ones for the
camels, shorter ones for the sheep.

Children route the camels back to their tribal
group. In the distance more herds string single file
around the edge of a salt flat. The night's rain has
rendered the *sabkhah* too wet for camels to cross.

Two herders roll their *thaub* (long garments)
to the waist and balance on the uneven stones of
the casement rim. One drops a leather bucket on a
long rope into the deep well. The laden bucket rocks
and spills on the ropes, as the two men haul it up.
Bright as diamonds in the sunlight, the falling drops
of water dive into the black depths. The child in the
rose print dress leans far out above the open well.
She extends her hand to the water, catches a pool
of falling drops, and flattens her palm against her
lips. The small brother barely reaches the top of the
casement. He laughs and jumps with excitement.
"Selma! Give some to me!" Cyndy watches,
wondering. It looks like fun—but, it is only water.

With words from the Koran, "Allah—the
Provider—the Merciful—the Giver of Life", chanted
in unison, bucket after bucket of water is brought up
from the well and emptied into a tall *haudh*. Water
spills on the limestone rocks, the sand about the

casement, the ground beneath the *haudh*. The
camels watch and sniff, but they do not drink.

"Great is the Goodness of Allah!" Another
bucketful emptied.

"Drink, you thirsting daughters of the desert!"
The lips curl, soft flesh rolls, but heads do not bend
to the water. The herdsman drops his bucket and
jumps down to the *haudh*. His cupped hands scoop
up the brackish liquid and toss it into the faces of
the nearest camels.

"*Miyah*—mother of camels—*miyah*!" he shouts.

The long, rough tongues search, taste, feel the
lubrication in their mouths. Heads lower to drink.
How long will it take to water them all? Time is the
rising and setting of the sun—the length of shadows
between prayers.

Beyond the well, Russ converses with a herder,
who helps a boy fasten a load of water onto the back
of a couched camel. "Why do I come to the desert?"

109

Top left: The child in the rose print dress helps bring the camels to water at Al Hinnah's remaining potable well.

Bottom left: A herdsman balances on the stones, as water pools about the casement and drips from the camels' lips.

Below: Salim instructs his son in the way of Bedu life, for one day the oil will be gone.

the man is saying. "To school my sons in the life of the Bedu. The oil in my country brings many *riyal*, but the desert has been here a long time. It will be here after the oil is gone."

"El, meet Salim," Russ says to me. "He works at the fire station in Abqaiq."

"The oil will not last forever," Salim says. "Then, what will my sons do? They want to work for the oil company. They do not understand today is but a passing moment in history, that one day they will be left with a *dirrah* and nothing more. First, learn to live on the desert, to accept the destiny of Allah."

The day of tomorrow sits on the dunes, but, as I watch Salim's deft fingers tie the heavy rope into knots, I do not know how different life will be for him and for his sons, how deep modernization will penetrate. Desalinization—irrigation—agriculture—new cities and roads—communication—industrial complexes: Arabia of the 1980's will leave little to remember of the Saudi Arabia of 1963.

The gush of oil has placed me beside this ageless well. So technology will change herders and nomads into industrialists. And what will happen to the

bait ash sha'ar? Will they become curiosities, seen only in museums? Am I bringing an end to thousands of years—me with my open face and my camera? I feel a pressure to hold this now, even as the Bedouin. To escape responsibility, even as he shrinks from change.

I call the girls. We have lingered too long with these herds. A goodbye to Salim, and the truck and the Rover take off.

Jabal al Ahass—a site we have found in our search for other sites: Al Wannan, As Sarar, Al Ma'aqala. This ragged, solitary bulwark that blocks the open terrain is meaningless without its connotations known only to the Bedu: a junction of passing caravans, a gathering point of warriors, a site of deeds. For us the butte has one significance: memorize its details for recognition should we return this way.

We follow the churned course of the Darb al Kunhuri. Off to the right we see a flapping roof supported by two poles. Not a tent—just a temporary shelter for an old man, several women, and a number of children. Household goods and rolls of

Top: Household goods clutter the ground about a temporary shelter, as a woman hastens to arouse her sleeping relative: "Strangers have arrived!"

Bottom: Obedient to her mother's wish, Latifa steps outside the tent and faces me.

Below: The husband is amused by my questions, but I see only the Bedouin girl's beautiful eyes.

roofing clutter the ground. Dee, in the lead, observes and drives on. I look at Russ, expectantly.

"We're not stopping here," he says. "Not with all those women out in the open."

Neither dog, nor donkey, men, nor boys. "What if they need something?" I say.

Russ stops the car short, and the wheels spin up powder. "Looks like they've stripped camp for moving," he says. "I'll let you out and wait with Dee."

I head for the shelter. Cyndy runs from the truck and catches up. Together we circuit rolls of black

Al Wannan—a ragged tree, a crumbling wall and a well dead of sand—lives with the deeds of warriors.

worsted, metal trunks, blackened pots, the coffee box, camel saddles and scattered tentpoles.

"Hello—*as salaam alaikum*," I call, as Cyndy and I stand in front of the shelter. The old man leans on his cushions. A young woman with beautiful eyes sits next to him. Caught by strangers in the act of breaking camp, he is in no position to offer hospitality, especially with all the women exposed to view.

"Do you need help?" I say. "We have wheels."

His smile is amused, tolerant of foreigners who know nothing of his desert. And my world links with theirs, through yesterday and tomorrow, for I have betrayed the footsteps of the camel.

"The truck will be back," he says. "Where are you going?"

"Well, I'm not sure. To some place called As Sarar."

The old man's gaze is penetrating. He leans lower into the striped blanket on which he reclines. "You cannot go there," he says. I wait, puzzled. "You must have a pass. It is Bin Jalawi country."

A woman, aroused from sleep, joins the group. She calls out, and her mask rises as with the wind by the excitement of her breath. What has happened? Oh, strangers—a woman and a child. She steps from the shelter and faces me. A little girl rushes into the folds of her skirt.

"*Marhaba* (hello)," she says to me, holding the child by the hand. "You are an American?"

"Yes. We stopped to see if you needed help."

"No. We are just waiting. You are very kind."

On the desert, one builds a pyramid of stones to advertise a kindness. "See, all of you who pass by, this pile of stones honors a stranger who offered me a kindness." Now, on impulse, she pushes the child toward me. The little girl stands outside the canopy, pale hair stiff with dust, fingers twisting the cloth of her dress.

"*Allo—marhaba*. What is your name?" No answer—only a quick looking back for a mother's nod of reassurance, and a gesture to move closer. A name is spoken: "Latifa".

Obedient to her mother's wish, the child comes closer. I drop a piece of candy into her palm. The tilt of her small head straightens, and a sob surges. Sudden tears roll down both cheeks, and dropping the candy, she rushes to her mother.

The man smiles, not with pleasure, merely affirming previous conclusions: what do you expect from foreigners—what do they know of us? But the mother sends her child again. She is building her pyramid, not of stones, but of the startled beauty of her child's eyes.

I am used to being stared at by Bedouins, but I cannot deal with the plea that lingers in the tear-stained face. Some void hangs between me and Latifa—perhaps more candy, for the brother. She will not take it. The light in her eyes flickers, as the mist gathers and spills over the rims. The wetness on her cheeks is not splashes from a bucket for the joy of children.

Who holds the answer that I do not know? The *athl* tree does and the amused glance of the old man. I avoid his stare and turn toward the young Bedouin girl beside him, whose watchful eyes reveal nothing. Eyes of beauty accentuated by a black frame.

What king wouldn't tremble at their sight? What need to see more? The eyes are enough clue to all hidden feminine charms. To marry them would make the unveiling a moment of intense excitement. What is her relationship to this scraggly grey-beard?

"Your daughter is lovely," I tell him.

He shrugs. The women smother giggles. My disgrace deepens. I have nothing more to lose: "Your wife?"

The girl stirs. Her eyes give me the answer, as she smoothes the hair of a small boy between them.

"And—your son?"

This he acknowledges. A son. I touch the Hasselblad. Again the man shrugs. "*Tafaddali.*" Please yourself.

The camera sees the old man and the exquisite

eyes—reflecting an inner peace, undisturbed by any need to respond.

"She is so young to be his wife," I tell Russ when I return. "You should drive by just to look at her." But, of course, he will not, and Linda protests indignation at such an alliance.

"I bet she didn't have anything to say about it!" Linda says.

"Probably not," her father confirms. He expatiates on tribal affiliation, the well-being of the whole, the overnight bride of a king to cement alliance of tribes. "As Sarar *hinaak?*" (over there) he calls out to the old man.

The man rises and approaches the car—man to man. "Follow the Darb al Kunhuri."

"You need help?" Russ asks.

"No. Tonight we leave. The truck has gone for gasoline." Then, an after-thought. "You give us some?"

"Sorry. No extras. But I can give you a lift."

The Bedouin shakes his head, his freedom bound by the truck that will not get up and go with the rap of a camel stick. We wave goodbye, leaving the family lost behind a screen of dust.

"How come we haven't seen any tents?" Cyndy breaks the long rattling of the car.

"Can't ever be sure we'll find any," her father says. His hands are tight on the wheel. The sand is deep and soft. The Rover grinds, swerves, grabs for a hold. There has been no rain here. Russ takes to the *dikakah.*

As far as we can see—nothing. No camels, no black line of a *bait.* Only dry brush, the ash of summer's kiln. There must be areas of this great desert so isolated, so distant that gasoline and cars are but the toys of children. We nibble at the edge. The family with the truck could not go there and must settle.

At As Sudayrah the wind covered our tracks and laughed. It cannot cover them any more, for others follow—the new track of the Bedu. Materialism, the force that arrives with us, steals from the Bedu the openness and freedom of distant deserts. Already it shows: the nomad's truck, the glint of a hair clip beneath a veil, a transistor radio to sweeten the waiting. One will no longer answer the call of thunder, or notice the scampering of a tiny scarlet spider, Daughter of the Rain.

Our wheels lay down our guilt. We are of this truck. We must turn back before the Sheikh halts

his people to try on for size this lifestyle we are putting up for sale—and today it is years too large.

From the top of the rise—trees. Grey, dusty tamarisks.

Our approach reveals not an oasis but a few stunted trees and a well full of sand. And flies! Others have stopped here more recently than when the well died. We have not happened across something new. We, too, need shade and to set up for lunch.

"Yes, sir," Dee says, fixing Cyndy a peanut butter sandwich. "I'm sure this is the place—Al Wannan." Like the Bedu, Dee spins a tale of heroes—of a horse that ran all the way from Al Wannan to Kuwait, a distance of two hundred kilometers. "'Course, she dropped dead when she got there, but that's what my Saudi boys tell me. Yes, sir. Ran all the way."

"Sharifah could do it!" Cyndy says. Dee ruffles her hair. "So you think your little ol' mare is pretty good, don't you?"

The tumbled casement of this old well, its stones snared in tangles of dry stalks and rags of palm fronds, contains more than sand. It holds the deed of a hot-blooded pony, a bridle of colored wool framing her tawny mane, strings of orange tassels swinging against her chest. A last drink from the well, and she is off, wide-set eyes wild, nostrils opened, hooves skimming the ground. On and on . . . The flare of a campfire! A hitch in the rhythm as she changes leads, but the rider holds firm. "Oh, Daughter of the Wind, heart of Saqlawi, pride of the Bani Khalid, look not to rest at the *bait ash sha'ar* but fly faster than the lightning to the Wells of *Subaihiyah.*" I hear it all—in the brittle and broken fronds that rasp in the breeze.

Russ is saying: "This area of the Eastern Province is historical country. Many tales relate Ibn Saud's struggle for peace among the tribes. Particularly with Dhaiden al Huthlain, Paramount Sheikh of the Ajman."

"We've met many friendly people from that tribe," I say.

"Today. But thirty years ago, warring was a way of life, and the Ajman were ruthless fighters."

Thirty years! No more distant in time than this well from where I stand. What are we doing here, searching out secrets, bringing the past to life? The old Bedu said we needed a pass—that this was Ibn Jalawi country. Abdullah bin Jalawi—paladin, prince, fighting alongside his cousin Ibn Saud for peace and a better way of life—was Governor of Al Hasa, now the Eastern Province. This spot where we stand was once alive with camels, mares, and warring tribesmen.

"Why did we need a pass?" I ask.

"Probably a hangover from controlling the tribes. It would fit in with the story." I beg Russ to tell us more. "Take too long," he says. "We'd best move on, if we expect to make the time of that mare!"

"To Kuwait?" Cyndy says.

"No—to Al 'Uwaynah."

Beyond Al Wannan, the land opens into a wide pebbled valley. To the north, outlines of *jabal* and brush fringing extensive *sabkhah*. Nothing could exist there, yet tracks skirt the damp salt flats, dark against the dry sand.

"Sarar should be somewhere on our right," Russ says, studying the way. But I see nothing.

The fear of being lost never really disappears. The image of the valiant sorrel mare fades against the threat of a mire, too hazardous to cross. Grey etchings of forsaken *athl* trees scratch the horizon. Yet, somewhere there are good wells, for the Wadi al Miyah, Valley of Waters, is no legend of the campfire. When we reach it, we will find As Sarar.

Russ and Dee consult the compass. "Not going to attempt those *sabkhah* with rain threatening," Russ says. "Let's head south toward 'Uwaynah."

Ominous thunder clouds and streaks of black indicate rain falling behind the high escarpment to the west. The pebbled landscape takes on new dimensions of monotony, and the afternoon wears on. The clouds close in, and with them the escarpment: guardian of history, keeper of secrets asleep in this vale.

Without warning a tire blows. The Rover's horn is a weak bleat. The truck continues ahead and sinks into the vastness of the land. First drops of rain spatter the windshield, as Russ leans into the last bolts and drops the jack. "Don't like the look of those clouds," he says, as Dee returns with the girls. "A place like this could wash out in a hurry." Dee agrees we'd better find high ground and camp. It is early, but, as Dee says: "Never could tell a cloudburst how to tell time!"

"Come on, young 'un," he says to Cyndy. "And bring that sweet potato pipe of yours."

"It's a tonette, Dee," she says.

Russ leads east, toward the sandhills—to higher ground protected by low dunes hanging shoulder to

shoulder. The storm moves fast, up from the south and bringing a darkness dense as night. I rush to set up lanterns, the Swedish butane stove, the pan of spaghetti to heat for dinner. Dee, Russ and Linda spread the tent for raising. It cannot be held in the rising wind that precedes a rush of rain. Weighting the tent with rocks, we all take shelter in the Rover. The double roof echoes the pelting water that rushes in sheets down the windows.

"How are we going to cook dinner?" Cyndy says, reclining in the back of the car on her sleeping bag.

"Dinner? You ain't hungry, are you?" Dee says. "Just bet I can rig up the best cold spaghetti you ever tasted—and orange juice!"

"Ugh!" from Linda.

"And, while I'm at it—how about a tune from that sweet potato pipe?"

"Dee! It's a tonette!"

I drift to sleep against the chill of an unopened sleeping bag, Linda's head on my lap. The high voice of the wind and the rain still falling merge into children's laughter, as they reach out to catch the diamond drops.

The desert after a rain! A hot breakfast, and we feel like new. Linda waves from the top of a sandhill. Cyndy comes racing down. "Hey, Mom! Tents—a really big one!"

Russ and Dee are packing up the cars. "See any men?" Russ asks.

"Only one—kinda old," Cyndy says.

His look is one for caution, as the girls and I head for the other side of the hill, where a shepherdess collects sheep to graze, and children set out to gather the desert brushwood, from kilometers afield. The large tent is built on four poles, instead of the usual three, signifying the *bait* of a *sheikh*. The face is open to the morning air and all within visible. Two elaborate *qata*, like paintings on a wall, designate a three-pole area for the *mahram*. And a real kitchen—the overhang! No pots, nor pans, nor waterskins in the parlor! We were still asleep when breakfast was prepared here—lightly soured camel's milk rocked in a goatskin.

A woman stands by the tentpole of the *mahram*, watching me. She is Nejela, wife of the *sheikh*. In the absence of her husband she upholds family traditions of hospitality. She gives me the grand tour of her house, omitting the *majlis* where Dee and Russ are conversing with a herdsman. The *qash*—a wall of piled quilts, mattresses, sacks and saddlebags

Nejela, wife of a *sheikh*,
upholds traditions of
hospitality and invites us to
take a tour of her house.

—is built against the *qata* to further separate the *majlis*. The *maksar* fills the place of honor in the center of the *mahram*. Then, there's a rifle, trunks, fine rugs, a loom, an infant's leather hammock, and the stores. Children play hide-and-seek about her skirts. A lamb sniffs her feet. She is Nejela—*umm al aiyal*, mother of the children.

She watches as I avoid a pile of refuse gathered up from the floor. "Tomorrow we shall go, *inshallah*,"

she says. "To the grasses my husband brings back with him."

"Will it be far ?" I ask.

"He has been gone two sunset prayers."

This *bait ash sha'ar* indicates a man of wealth. His tribal division will count many camels, his family numerous. Nejela invites me to join her on the Persian rugs and embroidered cushions of the *mahram*. Older girls serve tea in small gold-rimmed

glasses. *Shaay*—tea, hot and sweet. The girls' giggles are as sweet as the tea. Their skirts swish, as they squat, scattering sand. I am at home with the women and children of the *bait ash sha'ar*, the worsted roof, the smell of salt and sand, the pungency of animals, the fragrance of tea.

"There are Bedu in America?" Nejela asks.

"Oh—no!" I am caught off guard. A caravan of camels and tents swinging down the freeways!

She removes a ring from her finger, heavy silver with large turquoise stone, and leaning forward,

slips it on mine. "It is for you," she says. Her wandering fingers touch my plain wedding band, but her eyes are elsewhere. She fingers the high sheen and brilliant color of my splashy nylon skirt. She wants something. A gift for a gift? A bell bracelet for an aspirin . . .No, Nejela wants a trade. My gold earrings from Beirut are the equivalent of the large ring, but she doesn't want them. The reciprocal gift should be of greater value than the first. Her fingers touch my wristwatch.

"I may not give it," I say. "It is a gift from my husband."

"But it is yours, and he will give you more." Her response is quick. "*Kulla wahid*—it is all the same."

"No. This one is for love." I study her eyes. "Do you love your husband?"

She shrugs. "*Ma laish . . .*" It doesn't matter.

What does Nejela know of the interaction of a man and a woman? Her girlhood has permitted no association with males, other than father and brothers. She marries a cousin—a stranger. Security lies in a natural response to a natural desire, and in the approval of family. She never goes to bed without her husband, always waits, and together they roll up in the red quilt on a thin mattress on the sandy floor. And, personal love? How much does it really matter? Love is a name— the family name—to honor for life.

A lot of chattering emanates from behind the Rover, where Linda and Cyndy are surrounded by many women and children. I go to their rescue and am accosted by an older woman. She wears an odd collection of veiling wrapped about head and shoulders. Like the changing casements of wells, the layers have risen with age. She wears no outer cloak, for old age is its own mantle. Time is in her hands, in her dress and in her voice.

"You have come a long way?" she asks. Her fingers twist coarse thread on her *maghzal*, the spindle, a tool that is never idle.

"From Dhahran."

She looks at the car. "It is better than the camel?"

"Yes. Faster," I say.

"But, it does not give milk."

"No. We buy food in the town and carry it in the car." I tell Linda to get out the sweet rolls and share them with the women.

"*Wajid riyal*—too expensive," she says, shaking her head. "It is a bad gift, this thing Allah has given you."

She pulls coarse animal hair into a thread—and she is sorry for me. She twists the thread on a simple stick, polished with long usage, from a hunk of sheep hair plugged into the split fork of a branch held under her arm. In all the passing years, there has been no other way. But the woman behind the years is the same as I.

Nejela smiles. She has been to Kuwait and seen many things, even if she does not understand them all.

Tonight the family will gather about the campfire to hear tales of greatness, retold by he who is the best storyteller: poetic, romantic, weaving all history into the moment. Tomorrow is history, too, when tales of warriors and camels may become those of trucks and gasoline. "Never was there such a *Jarbu*," Russ might relate. "Conquered all terrain—ate not, nor rested. Sad was its fate when it ran out of gasoline and died."

Cyndy nudges me, pointing out three women who stand side by side, watching us. "You can't tell them apart," she says.

"Yeah," Linda adds. "How does that little kid know which one is her mother?"

"You always find me when the commissary is full of women," I say.

"Yes—but we know you," Cyndy says.

"So does that little girl know her mother."

" 'Cause they're wearing the same dress?"

Bedouin family females are the original mother and daughter look alikes.

"Now, take their hands," I say. "Some are older, some younger; and their eyes: some clear and bright, others with wrinkles—like mine!"

"Really? You're wrong on that, Mom," Linda says, winging me a smile. "But now I can see that their *abayah* are not the same."

"That's right. The young one rolls hers to bring it farther back on her head—shows more of her hair that way. The middle one almost covers her forehead, and the third one is in between."

"Guess that's what you call individuality," Linda says.

"And that's how you distinguish one person from another," I add.

Cyndy sidles up and puts her arm around me. "I can always tell you, Mom."

"You can? How?"

"Simple—you're my mother!"

Bedu life weaves in and out of the tents and the land. The land is paramount. It is the *bait ash sha'ar*

Left: Cyndy asks: "How does that little kid know which one is her mother?"

Below: Bedu life weaves in and out of the tents, and the *bait ash sha'ar* leaves its patterns on the sand.

that leaves its life patterns on the sand: tufts of wool, ruptures from pegs and poles, a circle trampled, and the dung of camels, donkeys, sheep and goats. And before—horses.

When did the mares disappear from the tribes? The old man knows. He has seen it all, for he was a young man thirty years ago. Cyndy and I walk closer to him. He sees us coming and turns about to disappear inside his tent. We watch him return, pick up a lamb, and chase off a group of large ewes with his stick.

We are not of his era. We confuse him. He wishes no confrontation with us. Once he was not confused —he was a warrior and carried a rifle, rode a camel on *ghazu*, his mare tied to the camel's saddle. He was

as deft as any tribesman to change mounts and dash off in a surprise charge to raid an enemy. Sometimes it was a friendly encampment, chivalrously warned in advance. The shouting, the dust, the milling animals might be at his camp tomorrow. But today he is the conqueror, his the triumph, his the booty: today—thirty years ago. Perhaps he was one who challenged the forces of Ibn Saud in this valley.

Cyndy draws my attention to a horse's bridle hanging on the tentpole. It is braided of colored wool and decorated with tassels and cowrie shells, worn now and faded. "Maybe he's got a horse," she cries. "I'm going to ask Dad!"

I watch her bounce away in search of her father. No, Cyndy, there'll be no horses here. Those that

Top left: Thirty years ago he was a warrior and rode a camel to battle—today he wishes no confrontation with us.

Bottom left: A camel, a man, his son and daughter collect sweet water from a rainpool.

didn't run away became the booty of war.

I still wear Nejela's ring. She has not asked for it, but before leaving I offer its return. With a smile of "*Kulla wahid*" she puts it on her finger.

Our cars take off from the high ground into the valley. The morning's encounter urges us on to reach Al 'Uwaynah. Out of the flat openness appears an unmistakable difference: a huge camel. No, two camels and a man. Russ is willing to stop and cool the engine, so the girls and I head toward the distant group. Now, we see two children. My eagerness rushes faster than the stomp of my boots. Surprisingly, the man hurries to meet us.

"Hello! Hello! Where have you come from?"

"From Al Hinnah—yesterday."

"Did you see a red truck?"

"No—but we met a family waiting for one . . ."

"*Alhamdulillah!* That is good news. My brother will come."

The camels are the largest I have seen: massive heads, coats thick and curly. They are couched on the edge of an extensive rainpool. Goatskins and metal basins lie nearby. The skirts of the boy and the man are hiked up and knotted at the waist. The boy dips water from the rainpool and pours it into a goatskin. The girl is shy. A smile toys with her lips, then withdraws. Her bare feet are coated with drying marl.

"What is your name?" I ask. She looks at her father, finger shy against her lip. He encourages her. We are friends, he and I. We have met by chance, but I know we are friends. I brought good news: the brother will come.

"Muna," she whispers.

"What a large pool of water," I say to the man. "And it looks like more rain."

"The generosity of Allah is without bounds." He tells me his *bait* is east to the sandhills, and how he left early to collect the rainwater.

"Muna is very sweet," I say. "Do you have more daughters?"

"No—but, *inshallah.*"

"May I take her picture?" I raise the Hasselblad. His consent is one of pride. "On the camel?"

The father studies the great beast, uncertain. It appears content to rest against the cool dampness, but there is always that ingrained suspicion of an unwanted load—and she is so fragile, this Muna, against the backdrop of the camel's coat. He lifts Muna into the saddle and holds her hand against the pommel. I am fussy. His unattached hand will spoil the picture. Will he let go—just for a second?

Cyndy, too, must sit on the camel. "Thank you," I say, as our hands meet.

He walks a few steps with us toward the cars, his eyes observing the threatening rain streaks.

"We go to 'Uwaynah," I tell him in answer to his question.

"Great city of the Ajman," he says. "Many houses of hair—thousands of camels . . ."

"We must get there before the rain comes." I walk away, then turn to wave. Muna is running toward me. I wait for her to catch up. Her face, framed in gold braid, is raised to mine—expectation in the clear eyes, in the tilt of her head. I bend to brush her cheeks with my lips, for this time I do not fail.

Al 'Uwaynah, stronghold of the Ajman, city of *bait ash sha'ar*: a gathering place for warriors, families and herds. But our arrival discovers only an emptiness. The Bedu have gone, following the thunderheads to green pastures. Unnerving, the silence with only the blowing of the wind. A civilization has picked up and gone, leaving the land as bare as though it had never been.

We walk the gently rolling ground, lush green with blades of new grass. Low mounds of wells jut here and there, and in the distance the Darb al Kunhuri leads onward to Ma'aqala and Riyadh. The silence is filled with the noise of camp migrations: pulled poles and rolled roofs roped to pack saddles, the *maksar* strapped to beasts and arising with a lurch, the bleating of lambs tucked into saddlebags. At the signal from the Sheikh on his white *dhulul*, all move: the young cattle, the milk camels, the beasts of burden, the families. How did we miss it? The rains came before we did.

I sense the hurrying of women's footsteps where I stand, the drag of long skirts, trampled trails from children running, flattened circles where camels couched, caravans slipping into the night and leaving to dawn the silence of emptiness. Half hidden in the dust, I find a few orange and blue beads strung on a length of frayed string. How were they lost? Perhaps they belong to a child—a bracelet that caught on the frame of the *maksar*, as a man lifted her onto the great camel, and the beads dripped into the dust.

The ground swells about a dazzling wall of white limestone. Dee digs into the spongy resilience with

Left: She is so fragile, this child Muna in her embroidered *bukhnuq,* as she sits on the camel's back.

Below: Our arrival at Al 'Uwaynah, great tent city of the Ajman, discovers only an emptiness, for the rains came before we did.

the toe of his boot. "I've got a theory about these mounds," he says. They're built up of dung deposited by animals standing about the wells. The sun dried it out, and it got sifted through with blowing sand. More herds came, trod the first lot down, and added their own contribution to the pile."

"So in time the casements had to be raised," I say.

"Yup—that's what I figure," Dee says. "Now, look down there. See those grooves in the limestone? They're made by ropes."

We peer down into the depth of the well. The limestone blocks that line the sides seem to have no beginning, lost in the shadows where the sun slashes across the wall. Every layer bears worn grooves in the rock, for each was once the top of the well. I cannot count how many times the casement was raised. I cannot see that deep into the well, nor

pierce the secrets of centuries. But I sense the fluttering of a child's *bukhnuq* against the damp stones, as she leans out to catch the sparkling spills of water, bright orange and blue beads dangling from her wrist.

A few *athl* trees edge a group of low buildings. The only permanent structures of a great city. Through the blowing branches we glimpse a single *bait ash sha'ar.* Somebody has remained behind. I approach the tent alone. Support ropes tangle with branches, as they reach out for anchorage. The face is closed in, but a dip between curtain and roof reveals *arfaj* sticks piled high inside. Has the *bait* been left to keep sticks dry for others who come to camp? No—the Bedouin's tomorrow is today.

Eyes snag me as I peer inside, piercing through

Layers of limestone rock bear
grooves from ropes, for each
was once the top of the well.

An old woman of the Ajman
bargains with me to purchase
her unusual nosering.

wrinkled and drooping lids. A woman. She parts the
curtains and comes outside, revealing the floor
covered with sticks. She stands there challenging my
interruption of her solitude, like the ashes of a fire no
longer aflame, a well dead of sand. Her furtive glance
accepts I am alone.

From the depth of a pocket in her robe she
extracts two heavy silver bracelets. "You buy!" she
demands. The Bedouin bracelets are tubular, hinged
and heavy.

"How much?"

"Two hundred *riyal*!" Her voice is of other days.

She pushes me to buy, but they are too expensive.
I ask if her tribe is the Ajman. Beetle dark eyes hold
mine. The lids tighten, projecting thoughts through
a pinhole. She pockets the bracelets and disappears
into the tent. The click of a lock, the metallic
scraping of a lid. She returns; chains of silver and
strings of beads drip from her fingers. She puts them
in my hand: a circlet of gold, three inches across,
long chains of silver, a string of bright beads, a dome
of filigree silver fringed with bells.

"What is it?" I ask.

Her fingers fumble, as she slips the gold ring into a
link of short chain. She holds the ring close to her

nose, and the hook against the veiling that covers
her hair. A nosering! And gold.

"Where did this come from?" I ask.

"It is mine! Mine!" she almost shrieks.

"From where—'Uwaynah?"

"*La!*—no." She turns to the north and flings an
arm wide, as if indicating a great distance. She
gathers her skirts and hustles off, beckoning me to
follow. She stops, kicks at drift sand against a rock
wall. "*Fi sheikhah—sheikhah Ajman!*" she says. Did
the ring belong to the wife of an Ajman sheikh?
Perhaps lost, and this woman found it? I must have
that nosering—and a picture! My cunning matches
her own. I am as sly as Mohammed with my bracelet,
or Khalid's mother and the marriage contract. She is
amused. She and I have a kinship in the ring! I shall
buy the ring, and she must allow me to take her
picture with it. She agrees.

"What was her name, the *sheikhah*?"

"Ajmi—Ajmi!" I do not understand the rush of
Arabic.

Footsteps approach behind me. The Bedouin
woman dashes inside her *bait*, the nosering dropped
on the ground.

"Didn't I see a woman around here?" Dee says.

I pick up the fallen jewelry, now mine, its history
forever enclosed within the walls of a *bait ash sha'ar*.

From Al 'Uwaynah we return to the *sabkhah* of As
Sarar. Formidable and treacherous they ooze with
wet sand after the rain. Far distant of them, the tops
of trees are visible—As Sarar, but the *sabkhah*
prevent us reaching there. A consultation between
Dee and Russ determines a detour: drive the soft
sand to the base of the escarpment, then seek a
passage to the top.

I look back to the east—the way of Al Hinnah and
the Gulf. The Darb al Kunhuri is an old friend by
now. We know its shifting and turbulent way, but
we leave it behind, as the red truck follows the
Rover. Cyndy plays her pipe, bouncing with every
rut of the washed out sand.

"See that saddle?" Russ says. "The flat spot at
the top? I'm going to make for that."

An increased rise of the ground as we drive brings
the saddle lower. From the top, a ledge of sandstone
hangs half way down like a dropped bridge. Flood
waters have washed away the ground on either
side, but the center appears secure, held by boulders
balancing on puffs of sand.

"I'll go first," Russ says to Dee, as he locks into low gear.

The Rover makes a run for the top, but is stopped by large rocks and a grinding into wet sand just before the bridge. We roll back to the bottom. Four runs without success, but our tracks are packing the sand.

"Everybody out!" Russ says. "You take the truck first, Dee—you've got the heavier weight."

"Do you think we can make it?"

"I'm sure of it," Russ says. "But if the bridge cracks, I could make it with the Rover where you couldn't."

The red truck starts its run. "Play us a tune for luck!" Dee calls.

Cyndy pipes away: "I'm an Old Cowhand, from the Rio Grande . . ." The notes grind up in the roar of the truck's motor. The tires grip the sand, the motor strains, rocks tumble. The chassis jolts on the upper ledge, slips back, then—

"He made it!" Linda cries. "He's at the top!" She and Cyndy clamber up after Dee.

Russ climbs, too, inspecting the bridge. It is further undermined, a large crack running its length. If it should give way, the car would be thrown on its side. He examines the two large boulders that brace the bridge.

"El," Russ says to me. "Keep your eyes on those rocks as I go up. If they begin to move, holler!"

I crouch on the side of the escarpment, eyes to the boulders. One slips, as the Rover guns more power and jumps onto the sandstone bridge. I cry out, but Russ cannot hear. The Rover has sprung over the top.

The plateau is no more inviting than the land below. A tall peak rises in the distance, and on our right, the sheer drop of the escarpment. A few scattered camels—some black—are the only signs of life. We keep the rim of the escarpment in sight, but our way seems to be circling west. I ask Russ where he thinks we are.

"Difficult to say," he answers. "Can't relate our position to east or west."

"Why don't we give up trying to locate Sarar and just turn back?"

"Got to find it, now," he says. "Burnt up a lot of gas on that climb. I'm told there's some at Sarar—drum and ladle."

We continue in silence.

"We'll camp soon and get our bearings," Russ says, after endless driving. "At the minute we're in the middle of nowhere."

"Are we lost?" I ask.

"Well—wouldn't say that exactly. Just don't know where we are!"

We stand on the rim of the escarpment, Linda and I: not confronting the unknown, but accepting reality. In this awesome, overpowering wilderness—we are lost. Out of sight behind us, our camp is set. Smoke curls from the fire Dee and Cyndy are building, growing blacker as the light of day dwindles. Far out below—more distant than the eye can comprehend—an endless expanse of emptiness. All the nuances of proximity are gone in distance, fused into the immensity of the desert. Even the sun hastens to shorten its gaze on the forbidding land.

The unbroken theme of life repeats itself above the deeds of men. Somewhere as dusk falls, another man spreads his *ghutrah* in prayer. "Allah only is Great. Allah only is Life."

"How dead it all looks from here," Linda says. "But we have seen the desert live." She starts back to camp. "Come on, Mom. I'm sure Dee's got dinner ready by now."

We sit about the campfire, locked in an island of light. Now the storyteller is heard, weaving into the night the deeds of warriors.

"Well," Russ begins," . . . here's the story I promised. It concerns the Ajman, once the most powerful tribe in Al Hasa. Its *dirrah* includes the Wadi al Miyah with settlements such as Sarar and 'Uwaynah."

"But—we didn't see anybody there," Cyndy says.

"There's an old saying on the desert," Russ continues. " 'Where my camel stops, there rises a city', and that's how it is with 'Uwaynah. When we saw it, the camels had gone. Well, these settlements were permanent in the sense that they were home base, and tribesmen camped there during the long summer. Besides being a strong fighting force, the Ajman were politically influential. Their cooperation was necessary, if Ibn Saud was to hold his emerging Kingdom. Like other tribes, they were also fickle, siding for or against Ibn Saud on a whim. Mostly, they were motivated by religious reform—as were the 'Utaiba and the Mutair. They wanted to purify Islam of innovations."

"What does that mean?" Cyndy asks.

"Why—to take away the things that weren't

View from the escarpment
overlooking the Wadi Al
Miyah, site of tribal battles
during the unification of the
Kingdom.

there in the beginning. They became known as the
Ikhwan, the Brotherhood, and settled into
communities known as *hijra*. These religious
warriors were useful to Ibn Saud as a fighting force,
but their fierce independence made them unreliable
in their loyalties. The Paramount Sheikh of the
Ajman was Dhaiden al Huthlain. He often vacillated
in his acceptance of Ibn Saud because the King
leaned toward help from the west. Thus, booty
became a prime motive for joining a fight.
Sometimes, when Ibn Saud's forces fled to the rear
to regroup, the Ajman would attack their own side,
collect booty, then flee into the desert!"

"Pretty tricky," Cyndy says.

"How would you ever know who was on your
side?" Linda asks.

"Exactly," Russ continues. "The Bedu had their
own ideas. The King always hoped the tribesmen
would remember their promise of peace and looked
on them as children who would see the light.
However, from time to time he had to go after them
to teach them a lesson for their disloyalty.

"One time he caught up with the Paramount
Sheikh at the oasis of Hufuf, but that desert warrior
was ready for him. Huthlain sneaked off toward the
great dunes to the south, drawing Ibn Saud after
him."

Cyndy moves closer to Dee. "Hi, Dee," she says,
putting her hand on his arm. "Getting spooky, isn't
it?"

"The Ajman deployed their main force behind
the dunes, setting a trap. Ahead, a small group of
warriors led deeper into the sands. The strategy was
to isolate the King's forces without water. The

ululating cries of the Ajman women urging their men to victory drew the King forward. He could see their silhouettes, veils thrown off and waving great torches of *arfaj* that cast an orange glow against the sky. Ibn Saud found himself cut off. The Ajman rushed in, brandishing swords and screaming their battle cries. Ibn Saud's brother was killed and he himself wounded. He slipped away back to Hufuf determined never to be tricked by the Ajman again. Nor did he forgive them for the death of his brother."

"Did the King ever catch up with Huthlain?" Linda asks.

"Several years later," Russ says. "Dhaiden ultimately met death at 'Uwaynah. Again it was a confusion of chivalry and trickery. The wails of the women for their lost leader, and the glow in the sky from their flaming torches could be heard and seen throughout the Wadi al Miyah. After that, the remnants of the Ikhwan went north to join up with the Mutair."

"Yeah—" Dee says. "My boys talk about that story. Claim he didn't die in battle."

"However it happened, it was war—don't forget."

A breeze catches our fire. Dry sticks spurt flame and enliven briquets of charcoal. Somewhere a stone rolls.

Do not disturb the secrets asleep in this vale.

"That event wasn't very long ago," I say, sensing in the lonely night the ghosts of warriors.

"1929. Thirty-five years," Russ says. "In the spread of time, it could be tonight . . ."

Linda jumps up. "Thanks—a lot!"

"Where you sleeping, Dee?" Cyndy asks, hugging his arm.

"Right next to you—outside the tent! Somebody's got to keep an eye on those ghosts."

Russ and I take the flashlight and walk from the camp. On the edge of the escarpment we peer through the night at the vast emptiness below. "Just think," I say. "It all happened right here—in this loneliness where we don't belong."

Russ moves closer to the edge. "Wish I knew where we are—relatively. If I could spot Sarar down there, or 'Uwaynah, it would help. Maybe in the morning."

"Who do you think she was?" I say. "The woman with the nosering?"

"How should I know?"

"Stayed behind—with all those sticks. Maybe—

she remembers . . ."

A thin, shrill wail pierces the air, infinitely acute in the sterile silence. It dies, then rises again.

"A dog. Must be down in Sarar," Russ says, as he swings the flashlight back to camp.

Out here you can't tell where sound is coming from. But to me it is more distant than immediately below. It is thirty-five years into the past. Al 'Uwaynah! Old eyes behind a mask! A tent full of dried sticks! The ululating of women—the sweep of long skirts across the sand! I shake myself from this drift into fantasy and turn to follow Russ.

A luminescence lingers over the valley below, eerie in the darkness. There is no moon and scudding clouds blot the stars, phantom warriors riding into battle. A bat darts into the open from a break in the limestone cliff—its blind gyrations wheel like questions that have no answers.

PART VI
In Search of Black Camels (March 1964)

BEDOUIN WARRIORS' SONG
Peace upon you, oh folks who
Crave to punish the aggressors,
To stand against those who
Prove to be at fault.

We, the natives of al Oja,
Boldly penetrate the rising
Smoke, moving forward
Towards the wall of death,
For the foe hides there!

They were known as Ash Shurf, the honored ones, a unique herd of black camels isolated and guarded in their own grazing grounds. A rallying point in war— a proud possession in peace. And one day they were gone, secret grazing grounds deserted—even as the folding of a tent. And with them went the heart of a great tribe.

Was it truth or legend, this story of the black camels?

"Do you think we could make it to Qaryat al Ulya?" I ask Russ. Spring has come to the desert, and we are eager once again to pick up the footsteps of the camel.

"What's up there?" he asks.

"Well—I've been reading about it—an Ikhwan village—a *hijra*, once a settlement of the Mutair."

Russ turns thoughtful. "You don't know what you're asking. That's questionable territory." Peace rules the desert, but the deeds of warriors are not forgotten.

What are the Mutair like now? Once, they were a powerful tribe of Najd and Eastern Arabia, defiant, a law unto themselves. The Ash Shurf became the property of Ibn Saud at the time he defeated the tribe. How long does it take for wounds to heal?

What did the King do with them? Where are they now?

"I can tell you right now no tribesman will talk about it," Russ says. "Why—not so long ago you needed a *rafiq* to cross the *dirrah*." A *rafiq* was a tribesman who accompanied a traveler to guarantee safe passage.

"You don't know—we might find out something," I say.

"Perhaps more than you expect," Russ says. "The subject is still sensitive."

"We can take Sharif," Cyndy says. "Please, Dad. He'll protect us!" Sharif is our two-year-old Dalmation, offspring of champions, even to the black spots on his tail.

"We'll see," Russ says. "But you know *sharif* is the singular of *shurf*, noble. The lost herd and a dog having the same name won't go over so good. Arabs tolerate only the *saluqi*."

Once again, on a clear March day of 1964, we drive the Northern Access Road. Salt crystals

A herd of camels wanders across the sand, as we set off in search of the Ash Shurf, unique black camel herd of the Al Mutair.

132

sparkle in the *sabkhah*. Ash Sheikh glistens with golden glory, and Kilo 100 is a misty yellow with flowering *arfaj*. The turbulent flares of the Abu Hadriyah GOSP, the pump station of An Nu'ayriyah, and here the black top comes to an end.

We bunk in An Nu'ayriyah for the night and awaken for an early morning start. Gas tanks topped off, and a final salute to the last outpost. We maneuver close to Jabal An Nu'ayriyah, the unique formation that gives the area its name.

The *jabal* stands smooth and tall in the pale morning light, a series of peaks and saddles and leaning boulders. Small figures stumble toward us from the base. Black in the shades where the sun does not reach, they move forward into the sunshine: a boy, a mother camel and a calf. Black camels! We all see them at once. The calf stumbles and falls, double-jointed legs spread in all directions. It looks like an enormous spider. The boy throws his arms about the baby and pulls it up, setting the legs straight. Dee shouts, and Russ stops the car.

I approach the group slowly. The boy's eyes turn on me beneath his woollen cap.

"It's so little," Cyndy says.

"Don't let that dog out," her father cautions.

I step forward. "How old is the calf?"

No answer. He is trapped beyond escape, and his startled eyes betray his fear.

"You talk to him, Cyndy. Just say: *kam umrah*."

The boy's words are less than a whisper. "*Yawmain . . .*"

Only two days old! The mother brushes up against the calf and couches. The baby leans against her, uncertain legs sliding along her body to the ground and folding awkwardly. Mother and child stretch necks and rub heads together—body language.

"That's a fine camel," Russ says to the boy. "Do you have more black ones?"

"No."

"Where's the father?"

Silence.

"He doesn't know that," I say.

"Of course he does. The ancestry of a well bred camel is known to every Bedouin child— remembered, not written."

I ask him where his *bait* is, and he points toward the *jabal* with his stick.

"I have a camel stick," Cyndy says, Russ translating. "Only it's at home."

The boy comes alive, "Is your stick good or bad?"

"I don't know—I think it's good. Anyway, as good as yours."

"No. Mine is a good-bad stick."

"Why is that?" Russ asks him.

"*Shuf!*" the boy says. He tosses his stick into the air, catches it along the stem as it falls, then, fist upon fist until he reaches the knobhead, he repeats:

"Good stick—
Bad-good stick—
Good-bad stick—
Bad stick."

His last fist falls on "Good-bad stick".

"Well, I'll be darned," Dee says. "Used to do that with a baseball bat!"

But the boy has not finished, "Good stick I keep. Bad-good stick I keep until I get a better one. Good-bad stick I keep if I can't find any better. Bad stick I throw away."

"Hey—that's neat!" Cyndy says. "I'll try that with mine."

The mother is on her feet and moving off. The calf struggles to rise, and again the Bedouin helps it to its feet. Cyndy reaches out and runs her hand over the soft, curly coat. The calf bleats to follow its mother.

"You're lucky to have a baby like that," Cyndy says. The boy moves past her. His visage softens, as he guides the calf toward its mother. "Good-bad stick," Cyndy says, watching them go. "Yup—that's probably what I've got, too."

Two *bait ash sha'ar* are pegged to the slope of Jabal An Nu'ayriyah. From a distance we determine signs of early morning activity: a herdsman moves camels out to graze, pots and pans set out for cleaning, quilts airing along the support ropes, all faces open to the sun.

Russ pulls off the road and stops. Perhaps we can learn something here. A tall woman is the only person visible about the tents.

"Why don't I go first and see what happens," I say.

The road is some distance from the *jabal*. I start walking, slowly, apparently unobserved. As I approach closer, a man on camelback swings around the tent and stops. He makes no overture for me to continue. Concerned whether to retreat or stay, I become aware of the tall woman hurrying around the tent. She stands in the open, facing me: a formidable black figure, long barrelled rifle held

Two *bait ash sha'ar* are pegged
to the slope of Jabal An
Nu'ayriyah. Russ pulls the
Rover off the road and stops.

Below: Leader of her family
group, the woman accepts
me as the same and invites me
to sit with her in her *bait.*

Right: Silver arfaj wears a
crown of yellow blossoms, and
babies enrich the camel herds.

ready in her two hands!

Starting motors roar—Russ has seen her, too.
The Rover and the red truck crawl slowly to my
rescue.

We stand in confrontation—this woman of the
ancient world defending her home, and I, years
forward of her future. In the soft morning sun, the
dampness of night not yet dry on the yellow blooms
of *arfaj*, we communicate without words. I stand
forth the leader of wheeled vehicles, and she the
undisputed leader of her clan. What have I come
into? Should I make a rush for the cars?

She lowers her rifle, and with a broad gesture,
hails me to come forward.

Russ drives the car alongside. "Get in, and we'll
go. She looks like she knows how to use that rifle."

The man trots up. His greeting is curt. No
welcome here.

"We admired your handsome herds," Russ says.

Cyndy leans out. "Ask him if the baby camel is
his."

The man looks at her: two children, a woman,
two men—and a dog. A family. Behind him, the
woman waggles the rifle and shouts. The gesture is
not threatening, rather demanding immediate
response. Where once I saw only age and the
obscenity of a mudhole, confrontations are now
real. It is not Russ' Arabic that will resolve this
situation—but women. She with the gun—and I.
I respond to her gesture and walk ahead, the cars
following and stopping short of the tents.

The woman strides toward me, rifle erect. "Who
are you?" Her tone is curt. No graceful gestures—no
words like chains of flowers on a spring day.

"*Marhaba*," I say, equaling her strength of voice.
I hold the camera in my hands, as she her rifle. I, too,
have a weapon of importance. "We are Americans—
from Dhahran. We have come to visit the *dirrah* of
the Bedu."

There is no mistaking her dominance of the
group. She circles me, almost like a guard dog, and
I see a leather holster with pistol at her waist. No
fooling with this one! She throws words at the camel
rider, and he backs off, pursuing a pair of blond
camels.

"You are *sheikhah*?" she asks, indicating the cars.

Am I leader of this caravan on wheels? Oh, yes, I
tell her, for I can be no less than she. The woman is
pleased. The correct things have been said. No
arguments with her! I will agree to anything.

"*Tafaddali*—welcome to my *bait.*" I alone am
invited to step inside the *sheikhah*'s tent. Life goes on
inside the same as in any other—only one difference:
no *majlis*. No council of men about a coffee fire. She
is second to no man. She is *sheikhah*.

I am not sure how to handle her, but she sits with
me on the mat. We are equals. She asks if I have
large herds, but I tell her, no—my husband works
for the oil company, for the King.

"But you are *sheikhah*?"

"Oh, yes! I am leader of the family." Family—
tribe—it's all the same. I decide to change the
subject. "We saw a black camel calf—do you know
where there are more?"

"No more. The mother is best of my herd. I nearly

lost them both, but Allah takes care of his children."

"*Alhamdulillah*," I respond, praising Allah.

"The calf will not be born," she continues. "Its feet hang out. The mother groans and cries, but she won't let me help her—she wants to bite and kick."

Russ edges closer to the tent to see I don't get into trouble.

"Allah! Allah! It was the same when my husband died. I could not help him. It is in the hands of Allah!"

"I saw the mother. She is good now," I say.

"*Alhamdulillah*! The baby, like a wet rag, drops to the ground. I see pain in the mother's eyes. She is asking me to come. She has achieved this thing herself—she is *sharifah*."

"Like the Ash Shurf . . ." I prompted. "Of the Mutair."

She gets up. "They are finished."

"Do you know what happened to them?"

"Only Allah knows."

"We are going to Qaryat al Ulya—do you come from there?"

"No. From the sands."

People of the sands—of the bleak Rub' al Khali, true desert Bedouin, aligned with the Ajman. How far they have come to share the springtime grasses. She tells me it took three months to bring the herds.

I notice the sister preparing to make tea, and Russ signaling me from outside. He's tired of waiting.

"It's a long way to Qaryat al Ulya, and I must direct my family to leave."

Without persuasion she gets up, reaches for the rifle leaning against the tentpole, and steps outside to shout to a man who talks with Dee.

"This man is Mutairi," she tells me. "He will give you directions."

Dee climbs into the truck, taking Cyndy with him. Russ lags behind with the Mutairi. I slide behind the wheel of the driver's seat.

"Move over," Russ says, as he comes up and stoops to get into the car.

"I'm driving."

"What!"

"At least as far as the road. After all, if I'm *sheikhah* of this caravan, I've got to lead it out!"

"Well, that's a fine note," Russ says, walking around to the other side. He settles himself in the passenger's seat. "*Sheikhah*!"

The desert in spring has become a nymph. Her filmy gown of lavender and white floats above the sand, as she runs to meet the sky. All the wrath of wind and sun is now overlaid with silver *arfaj* that carries a crown of yellow blossoms, deepening to

137

gold against the dunes. Spring—a time for joy—a time for happiness—a time for babies!

The herds along the Tapline are rich with young —all fluff, and legs and bawls. Babies stumble after mothers, who linger over the rich fodder of delicate blooms. We stop for the sheer delight of running through beauty. Sighting *athl* trees, no longer dusty, we decide to have lunch. Dee jumps from the red truck and glances toward a stony ridge.

"Well, I'll be," he says. "That little devil's been following us all the way!"

"Who's that, Dee," Linda says, slamming the Rover door.

"You ain't seen him? That little yellow fox? Been trackin' us from a way back."

The tiny animal stands unmoving among the stones of the ridge, precision of pointed ears the only clue to his presence.

"Maybe he's hungry," Cyndy says.

"Don't you believe it," Dee says. "He finds plenty to eat out there. Now, take me—I'm starved!" He sets out the makings for sandwiches. "Yes, sir—that fox is the best little tracker in the desert. Say, did I ever tell you about the time I got accused of stealing camels?"

Everybody is busy spreading sandwiches, so Dee continues.

"Well, this old Bedu was out near the Abqaiq stables with six camels, as Sheikh and I—that's my old pony—came off the sands where we'd been ridin' all morning. This old guy said I'd frightened his camels, causing them to lose his saddlebag with Saudi Riyal 1000 in gold! I figured he'd never had any gold, and he was after me for a touch. Well, a few days later I got an order from the local *qadi* (judge) to appear in court. The man now claimed I'd chased his camels with my horse, and *they* were lost, too!"

"Why, Dee—you never told us!" I say.

"Well, I'm no tracker," Dee continues. "But I know every inch of that sand around Abqaiq. That old duffer was lying, and I had to prove it. So, I said to myself, if I was going to hide camels, where would I put them? Well, me and Sheikh had a little talk, then I saddled him up and off we went. Man, that little pony is fast—and smart. He picked up those camel tracks and sniffed out those beasts pretty as you please. Yes, sir—there they were in a fold of dunes! Six camels all tied together and two saddlebags! And, just as I thought, the old codger

confessed he didn't own a stitch of gold!"

"You could have gone to jail!" Linda says.

I encourage the girls to help Dee pack away the lunch, and then walk off with the camera to photograph some flowers. A camel with two riders, a girl and a boy, tops the hill ahead and trots down the slope. Near the tumbled stones of an abandoned casement, the girl slips to the ground and watches the boy ride away. The Bedouin maid gazes far afield—waiting. Impulsively she plumps down, her red skirt coloring the grass. She plucks a flower, removes her veil, and winds the stem in her hair. A man on camelback approaches from behind, his red *ghutrah* as challenging as her vibrant skirt. With a little cry she runs off, but he catches her and pulls her toward him.

A stolen moment of bliss among the camels! How can I retreat? The sharp barking of a dog rips the spring day, as a black and white body leaps toward the man's camel.

"Sharif!" I yell, "No!"

The girl screams. The man chases after his running camel. I want to stop it, but I can't. The desert drama plays on. Beating his camel with a stick, the boy rushes up, she jumps behind him, and they disappear over the top of the hill.

"You bad boy," Cyndy says, snapping the leash on Sharif. "You shouldn't chase camels!" She puts the dog in the car.

Russ is annoyed when I rejoin him. "Well—guess we'd better leave," I say.

"Too late for that," he answers. "Look."

The pattern of unexpected encounters with lone Bedouin women continues. Two camel riders again top the hill—this time the boy and a man. The boy points to the *athl* trees where we wait, and the man jumps to the ground. He starts down the slope, stopping to squat behind tall brush with each few feet of descent.

"What do you suppose he's up to?" Dee says. "He knows we can see him."

The flutter of veils and a red skirt appear against the clear blue sky. The girl crosses the top of the hill, her eyes searching below, but the man is gone. How bold she is—yet, the fold of dunes, the vales of stony ridges wait for lovers. For this, her sisters of the towns might be stoned.

Two-thirds down the slope, the man halts and settles down behind a bush. We wait, wondering what he's doing. I get the binoculars from the car,

An abandoned well with
tumbled rocks and wooden
frame where ropes were hung
to drop the buckets.

steady the glasses, twirl the focus ring, and search
the hillside. Suddenly, I know what the Bedu is
doing, for he and I come eye to eye, lens to lens, as
he catches me in the focus of his own binoculars!

The angry father walks to meet us with an agony
of affront. He appears gaunt and hollow-eyed, as
though perpetually hungry. The boy comes forward,
too. He wears a gold-stitched *kufiyah* (cap) grey as
his worn *thaub* lashed over shoulder and waist with
a length of rope. Both challenge us with their pride.

The traditional greetings from Russ elicit no
response. He tries again. "*Allah yusallimuk . . .*"
(God give you peace) An unwilling recognition
that this foreigner understands his language,
brings forth a curt nod and a begrudged greeting,
though anger rides the final word.

"Go. This is my country. I do not want you here."
Hadn't I heard such words before?

"We're just driving through," Russ says, ". . . on
our way to Qaryat al Ulya."

"Go back. It is not your country."

"Let's go," I say to Russ, conscious of the boy
who scowls at me. His faded *thaub* could be a gown
of crimson velvet, the frayed rope a sash of gold.
The wearing is in the eyes, in the set of the head.

"No," Russ says. "He could cause trouble for us."

I meet the boy's stare. He's not much older than
Linda, surely I can reach him. "*Marhaba*—what's
your name?" Only a grim staring ahead.

"Well," Russ says turning to me. "Seems we
scattered his camels and frightened his family.
Looks like we've come to a dead end."

Dee's story! We could be accused of anything.

"Tell him we're sorry about the dog," I say.

"That would hardly satisfy his damaged honor."

The boy watches me. Perhaps a kind word will
soften him. "*Marhaba*—hello, Mohammed."

The storm in the eyes disperses, driven off by
confusion and wonderment. "Your name is
Mohammed?"

"*Na'am*, yes. Mohammed." He turns away
quickly.

So, I was lucky—but not a difficult guess, for
Mohammed is the most common and honored of all
Arabic names. "Mohammed—you are Mohammed
bin Abdullah."

The boy looks sharply to his father. The man
stops berating Russ, eyes staring at me. I have
guessed well. The father is Abdullah. His penetrating
glance asks how we knew the names: it is not magic
nor the *jinn* but a wisdom granted by Allah. When he
turns to Russ, his voice is gentle. Mohammed, too,
relaxes, steals a glance at Linda.

"Don't know how you did it, El," Russ says. "But
the guy is pleasant. Even invited us to his tent! Keep
it up—we're not out of the woods yet."

"Mohammed, you have a brother. His name is
Said." There must be brothers, and Said is a good
name.

Shaken, the father implores Russ to come to his
bait—to partake of camel's milk as an honored
guest! I am even frightening myself! The brother
can't be Said, but he is! Russ insists we go to the
man's tent. It'll make us late, but avoid possible
trouble.

We get in the cars. Abdullah and his son will not
ride in the Rover with the dog and the women, but
jump in the back of Dee's truck. Bumping through
the *dikakah*, up and over the hill, robes flapping,
hanging on for dear life, the Bedouin father and son
guide us to their *bait ash sha'ar*.

It is a poor tent, small and in disrepair. The roof
sags and the rug is torn. The wife Sarah remains in
the small room with us, diligently pounding coffee
beans in a mortar while supporting a small boy at

Mohammed bin Abdullah
starts the fire at his *bait*—so
proud, his faded *thaub* could be
a gown of crimson velvet.

Right: Abdullah's tent is
patched and ragged, but the
warm camel's milk he serves
would please a king.

Far right: Mohammed returns
Ali to the broad rocker of his
mother's lap, while she pounds
coffee beans in the mortar.

her breast. Mohammed brings *arfaj* to start the fire sparking.

Two young boys watch just outside the tent. The girls, too, remain beyond the limits of the roof. In this poor Bedouin family, Sarah shares all with her man. Our coming does not change that. Besides, she is old, beyond complications with men. Abdullah calls over the *qata*, and soon a woman's bangled arm extends a bowl of milk. He pours some into a small pan, sets it on the fire to warm, then pours the milk into two small cups—for himself and Russ. I, who receive wisdom from Allah, am ignored.

"You must drink much," Abdullah urges, eyeing Russ' slender build. "It will make you strong!" Within the threshold of his *bait*, the most generous hospitality he can offer, poor as he may be.

Mohammed grabs one of the boys and pushes him toward me. "This one—what is his name?"

It is a game, now, and every game has a loser. But I shall try again. "I have told you—this one is Said."

Mohammed jumps with joy. "Yes! Yes!" He grabs the second boy. "And this one? What is his name?"

The dirty face—the dull black hair, not washed in how long—the grubby bare feet below a soiled *thaub* convey nothing. "Eeny—meeny—miney—mo . . ." Make a guess: "Why, your brother is Samir!"

Mohammed leaps up. "Yes! He is Samir!"

Without pausing, he grabs the baby from Sarah's lap. The damp lips purse, pulled from the breast. The

dark eyes stare. He is a large child, extracting comfort from the closeness of his mother. A sack of herbs is tied around his neck, keeping the child safe from harm.

"His name! His name!" Mohammed cries.

"His name is Rashid."

The chain is broken. I am no longer supernatural. The baby's name is Ali. How did I miss that one! Surely, now I must pay a forfeit.

Ali squirms and whines. Mohammed returns him to the broad rocker of his mother's lap. She lifts the skirt of his dress and gently touches his genitals. He curls toward her body. She gets up, squats outside the tent, surrounded by the other boys. She sets Ali on the edge of her knee. Firmer pressure on his penis, and he voids a stream, as she holds him away from her skirts.

I wonder on this closeness of mother and child— body close. A love that binds the sons.

My loss of luck—*hadh*—must pay a price. Balloons! Fill the tent with balloons. Linda gets a package from the car, and the two girls blow the crumpled sacks. Young eyes widen in disbelief, as the colored balls grow and grow. Freed ones skitter across the sand or burst on sharp stalks.

More! More! Samir is quick to learn that a lost one begets another. He takes his, runs off, and returns empty handed. What is he doing with all his balloons? I rise from my place near the fire and step outside. Bubbles of color rest inside the *mahram*. Oh,

141

Samir, you squirrel. But he wouldn't know that—only the ever present need to face tomorrow, and tomorrow there may not be any games.

Two women, one with a red skirt, squat outside near the *majlis*, listening to the conversation of men. I could not explain we have not betrayed a tryst.

I return to Sarah. "Such fine sons," I say. Her calloused feet, dark with henna, support the mortar, as she continues to pound the beans. The hard life of the Bedouin is in the weariness of eyes, the fatigue of muscles, the scarred hands, the body anguish of bearing sons, the remembrance of stones that mark a child's grave along the infinite route of wandering.

She has no concern for the world beyond her *bait*. Her response is to desert life: repair the tent and saddlebags, collect water and prepare new skins, build fires for meager meals, rock the daily *laban*, supervise the tasks of children and shepherds, care for the sick—and at night, the red quilt on a sandy floor. There is a quiet splendor in the dedication to tasks, in the consignment of personal identity to the tribal heap of anonymity.

The family is from Al Jafurah, to the south. They came seeking cousins in the *dirrah* of the Mutair and found them camped just beyond the ridge. Later in the afternoon, Sarah will walk there carrying Ali.

Left: Ali sits close beside his mother Sarah, a sack of sweet herbs tied about his neck.

Below: The girl in the red skirt sits near the *majlis*, listening to the conversation of men.

Abdullah and his family escort
us back to the cars, leaving
baby Ali to howl beside the
tent at the disengagement of
life's comforts.

The flowering desert, the open land, release from work—and to laugh with her sons at the antics of colored balloons—are the pleasures of her day.

It is Sarah who pours the coffee. The encrusted kettle, black and burned with ash, reflects her life: much used, deteriorating, yet continuing to flow and provide hospitality and pleasure shared in the desert brew.

The family follows us back to the cars, a swarm of blowing clothes and chattering voices: Abdullah, Mohammed, Said, Samir, Sarah, a red skirt, a woman with a spindle. And, standing arms outstretched in front of the *bait*, the baby Ali— wailing at the abrupt disengagement of life's comforts.

The terrain of flowering *arfaj* remains behind, and the cars traverse hard, rippled ground that is bare, rocky and flat. Here and there appear areas of tall brush. The stones go on forever, splaying out from under the tires. From these plains and ridges of the Summan, the *dirrah* of the Mutair spreads far to the north and west. It was at Artawiyah that Ibn Saud hoped to settle some of the Mutair, but the sword— not the hoe—became their tool.

The hard ground holds no tracks. There is no invitation to stop like an *athl* tree. Unexpectedly, the plains give way to rolling terrain, the loose, deep sand bearing imprints of many cart tracks. A massive, dun-colored fort marks the outskirts of Qaryat al Ulya. So—we have arrived. What now?

We traveled in search of an answer: What happened to the Ash Shurf?, but the distance in kilometers and centuries, the lonely desolation we passed through render the mind sobering. History encompasses the *dirrah* of the Mutair, but the tranquility and peace of this day absolve those who once marched as warriors, bearers of the banner of Ikhwan—religious zealots to whom western innovations were once offensive.

How long ago did the deeds and influence of Faisal Ad Dawish, Paramount Sheikh of the Al Mutair, fly like banners from towers similar to those before us? Instead of offering their support to the King, the desert warriors enforced their own rules, fiercely loyal only to themselves. Ibn Saud faced them, as he had to, with the sword, believing that right and the guidance of Allah would bring peace and unity to the country.

"I don't see anybody," Cyndy says, hanging onto Sharif.

The truck and the Rover huddle for a conference.

"There's a road around the last tower, and some shops—all closed," Dee says. "And a large well across from the fort."

"Okay," Russ says. "Let's pull over and wait."

A massive fort with crumbling
towers marks the outskirts of
Qaryat al Ulya. So, we have
arrived—now what?

Friday, the day to gather for community prayers,
is not a day for foreigners. We should have arrived
yesterday, but balloons and camel's milk made us
late.

The girls explore the surrounding area about the
high casement of the well, finding shards of pottery,
amber beads, glass bracelets and a cotter coin—a
tawilah, earliest monetary unit of Al Hasa. Green
and black with oxidation, the folded short metal bar
resembles a cotter pin and thus its name *tawilah*,
meaning long. How many encampments have
spread about this well over thousands of years? If
only one had time to dig! Archeology puts physical
pieces together to prove history. And stories—are
they not the building blocks of people that present a
personal record of what they were—they are?

Eight or ten boys converge on us. They shout and
jump at our group, keeping strangers at bay and
away from their women and girls. A well-dressed
young man arrives, speaking some English, and
asks if we are lost.

"Well, I don't know," Russ says. "We followed
some tracks that brought us here. Is this Qaryat Al
Ulya?"

"Yes," the young man, whose name is Faisal,
replies. "But the shops are closed."

"Mind if we look around?"

"*Ahlan wa sahlan.* You are welcome. I will show
you the way."

Faisal gets in the car and directs us around the
fort. Great wooden doors, studded with nail heads
and metal bands, hang askew, dragging the sand.
Once, long ago, the Turks made an agonizing march
to the sea. Now, instead of rifles and cannons, goats
wander through the junk of broken down cars. The
thick walls of marl blocks and flung *juss*—
fortification of the Turks against the desert's
unconquerable forces—now crumble under the sun
and wind.

The town's narrow streets are deserted. The
shops' rolled down metal shutters are anchored to
the ground by large hasp locks. No tree. No glimpse
of spring. The street ends at a square, alive with the
gathering of men, and here we stop. A large mosque,
of the same construction as the town, dominates the
area. Its arched entranceways and minaret angle
toward Makkah. Faisal leads Russ to a group of
elders standing against the wall.

More men and boys emerge from household
compounds behind high walls and press about the

cars. We cannot open the doors—nor do we wish to.
We would be swallowed up in the flow of cloaks!
The elders stare with suspicion: who stands in the
square of the Al Jum'ah Mosque, disturbing Friday
prayers? A vibrant chant rises above the town, as
the *muezzin* calls the faithful to prayer. Soon the men
are gone from the square, and we are alone in our
isolation as foreigners. We step out from the cars,
and a woman opens a door and smiles at us.

"Did you ask about the black camels?" I say to
Russ as he returns.

"No. Now is not the time."

We should have come yesterday—but how far
back into yesterday when there was another cry:
"The Winds of Al Jannat are blowing!" Battle cry of
the Ikhwan—"Come all ye who seek entrance into
Paradise!" I reach back into history and visualize an
army of warriors pushing beyond the square, down
the narrow streets, out onto the pebbled plain. A
thousand men! A thousand camels! Heady with
dedication, spiritual fanaticism, unable to
distinguish right from wrong. "Allah only is Great!"

Allah stands supreme on this square. We cannot
change ourselves, but we can respect the right of

145

Soon the men are gone from
the square. We get out of the
cars, and a woman opens a
door and smiles at us.

Faisal, a well dressed young
man of the town, approaches
the car and asks if we are lost.

privacy. I propose we leave, overwhelmed by a
sense of intrusion.

"It's up to you," Russ says. "The men are
gracious but not enthusiastic about our being here."
A final aristocratic figure floats against the mosque
wall, the Koran—soul of Islam—a treasure in his
hands.

Fanaticism of the Ikhwan has gone from this
village, the full beauty of Islam returned. But, 1929,
only thirty-five years before, the battle of Sibillah
and Ibn Saud's defeat of Ad Dawish—there must
be those who remember.

Russ starts up the motor, and Faisal comes
running. "You must not go!" The chanting of
prayers rises from the mosque. "I heard your family
speak of the Ash Shurf. After prayers the elders will
gather. You are invited to join them. They will tell
you what they know."

History and legend are wrapped within the walls
of a *bait ash sha'ar*. The elders gather in quiet dignity.
A circle forms about the coffee fire. Russ is there,
alien element opening wounds afresh, and I wish I
had not brought him to this.

I wait outside, where small boys play at horses
around the tent, dodging a little girl who drags a
goat by the ear. These grandchildren of warriors—
did their mothers know the Ash Shurf, drive the
herd ahead of warriors to victory? Did the black
camels exist? We saw some spotted throughout the
eastern deserts—an incidence of rare color, or
descendants of a unique herd? What will Russ
learn?

Coffee is brewed and served in solemn dignity.
Pungent cardamom excites the air. The refreshment
of declared faith heightens devotion to peace. The
deeds of tribal warriors join the circle in
remembrance.

"I came to speak of the Ash Shurf," Russ begins.
"We are interested in their history."

The eyes of the elder grow thoughtful: the Ash
Shurf—black, all black from their heads to their
hooves. How handsome they were! What pride of
possession! He had been at Artawiyah when
Ikhwan warriors brought home their leader
wounded in battle. He remembers the heaving
horses swinging to a halt near the well, how
weeping wives and daughters cared for Ad Dawish
and miraculously he recovered. Renewed strength
brought arrogance and fearlessness. The battle cry
came to life: "The winds of Al Jannat are blowing!"

Only this time Ad Dawish went down to defeat. To
the victor belongs the booty . . . Yes, the last time he
saw the black herd was when the women of Ad
Dawish, in traditions of chivalry, themselves true
desert warriors to the last, walked forth with the
Ash Shurf behind them to acknowledge the victor—
Ibn Saud.

The elder remembers the ringing words of Ibn
Saud that brought peace to Al Hasa and to Najd:
"From this day forth we shall lead a new life." And
the new life is good.

The sun still blazes down upon the land. The
breeze blows as the wind of Paradise, swirling the
sand, driving it against rock and dune. Its call is
powerful. It fuses the old days with the new. Within
the walls of Qaryat Al Ulya, dignity and pride cloak
men tighter than mantles. The past is the past—
today the land is free.

The coffee pot is drained, words of farewell
spoken, and we drive off in silence, the search for
black camels sobering. Faisal had warned Russ not
to inquire further—the subject is still too "political".

Some distance from the town we stop to let Sharif
out—he'd been shut in the car a long time.

"Did you find out anything?" I ask Russ.

147

History and legend are
wrapped within the walls of a
bait ash sha'ar, as the elders
gather in quiet dignity.

This grandchild of warriors—
did her mother know the Ash
Shurf, drive the herd ahead
of warriors to victory?

"Nothing, really," Russ says. "Evasive tactics
that led nowhere. One man said he knew them, that
they are still to be found, everywhere. It appears Ibn
Saud kept the herd until the Ikhwan settled into a
peaceful life. Then he divided the animals among the
tribe. The traditional distribution of booty."

We decide to return a different way, for fear of
being followed. We head south. The route should
approach the *sabkhah* near As Sarar. Tired and
hungry, we stop to eat and later camp some distance
along the way. Piled stones and large boulders form
an irregular wall of protection from the wind. Cyndy

We decide to return a different way, then tired and hungry pull up close to an *athl* tree to eat.

A young herder and his camel stop to watch us, as we follow along after Ahmed in his Jeep.

hunches beside me with the dog. His forelegs are on her shoulders, paws wrapping her neck, as he plants wet licks across her face.

"Gee. Mom, aren't you glad we brought Sharif? He'll be a good watchdog."

I pat the spotted coat and get whipped by an ecstatic tail. He'd never be a match for the fierce watchdogs of the *bait ash sha'ar*. "Better tuck him in your sleeping bag with you," I say. "That way you'll hear him when he barks."

Morning reveals the land caked and dusty. Powder churns under the wheels, and vegetation is desiccated and brittle. Even the Bedu shun the area known as "Bad grasses", "Poisonous water". We follow an escarpment, ravined and eroded, and after that—we do not know. Without warning—there it is. Another car! A jeep. A man in *ghutrah* and *thaub* hails us.

"*As salaam alaikum.*"

"*Wa alaikum as salaam . . .*"

Whatever the horror of the land, there is always the peace of God. The Jeep is stalled. The man understands that foreigners know how to revitalize the motor—though was it not Allah who provided this fortuitous gift? A lift of the hood, and Dee's

experienced eye spots a chewed fan belt. The red truck carries an assortment of replacement parts, and the Jeep is soon ready for the road again.

Ahmed al Ansari explains he started from beyond Ma'aqala yesterday and is going to As Sihaf to visit his family. All that way—alone, I think. What if we hadn't come by? Doesn't he understand that our vehicles are vulnerable to his desert without the means to repair them or smooth roads to drive on?

He asks where we are going, and Russ tells him "Ras Tanura". "As Sihaf is on your way," Ahmed says. "You must stop and rest with us."

We follow the Jeep, since Ahmed has come this way before, and finally reach the edge of a large *sabkhah* that borders the Bedu village of As Sihaf. Many people come running to meet us, but I see only one—the woman standing in front of the *bait ash sha'ar*—watching the girls and me approach. The brilliant red of her light silk dress fires the shadows, and gold embroidery glitters with her every move. Sunlight catches the sparkle of veiled necklaces and beads, and jeweled *jumkhas* with tiny bells that hang from her hair. It is her haughty stature and challenge of eyes that arrest me, for she appears a Scarlett O'Hara of the tents.

Cheese cakes crack and dry on a bush, strips of meat cure in the sun, and scraps with sugar collect flies on the ground. But—she is none of these . . .

Other women greet me warmly, and boys ask for their picture to be taken. I comply, hoping to catch the haughty vision in red in the background. Aware of her worth, she retreats to the shadows. But, as I sit with the other women sipping tea, a rustle of silk and jingle of bells alert me to her presence.

"Do you want my picture?" The voice is deep and slow.

We step outside, and she poses just short of the long rope that holds the roof at the *majlis*. I focus the lens.

"Fifty *riyal*." Scarlett says.

I expected it, and my answer is prompt. "No!"

The women watch, interested. They asked nothing, and I cannot insult them by purchasing beauty. Yet—the red dress, and wearing her dowry in gold are customary for a bride and draw me to her.

"Forty-five!" She catches my arm, as I start to turn away.

"Well—thirty-two," I say. "That's final."

"You must give me forty—no less!" She is upset

I maneuver the boys to the tripod where meat dries, hoping to catch the haughty beauty in the red dress in the background.

A woman wearing a polka dot head covering could be a townswoman of As Sarar—perhaps even a Persian.

now—almost furious—and her voice rises in pitch.

I, too, raise my voice. "No. It is too much."

"I want forty!" Her voice is a shout. An order.

A man rises from his place on the floor of the *majlis*. He bangs his fist across the rope that holds the roof. The tent shakes with the blow and the anger of his words, as he shouts at the *hareem*:

"Speak no more! Your tongue dishonors my tent and insults a guest. Go—perform prayers to Allah!"

Scarlett backs off. Her husband—Ahmed's father himself—has spoken! No *sheikh* of the silver screen has swept her off her feet, no fantasy from One Thousand And One Nights, but desert reality. I sip tea, knowing she is watching me. From the *qash* she takes a small prayer rug and sets it on the ground in the direction of Makkah. A man's red *ghutrah* lies on the wall of stores. She takes it and drapes it across the side of her head that faces me. It is heavy and falls off. She replaces it. Her features are hidden from my sight, as she loosens the mask and allows it to fall. Nothing obscures her from God, as, kneeling, she touches her forehead to the ground.

Time moves on with the conversation of men, with dates dipped into a bowl of milk where mounds of butter float, and with the second prayer of the day. As the men step out from the tent and face Makkah,

we say our farewells and drive off into the desert.

A patch of blackness ahead becomes a large flock of sheep. An old man, arms outstretched, forbids the passage of the cars. A woman standing in the midst of the sheep wears a polka dot head covering— different from the black of the *bait ash sha'ar*. She must be a townswoman of As Sarar—perhaps even a Persian.

"Where is your pass?" the man asks Russ.

"We are just driving through. We do not require a pass."

"It is the law of bin Jalawi! You must have a pass from the Governor!"

What is here that bin Jalawi needs to protect from strangers? Tribal wars are over. We do not come with mounted warriors and guns—only daughters and a spotted dog.

The woman and I exchange glances, each unusual to the other. A small girl in a peaked bonnet cries to be lifted up. The woman brushes her off— she already carries an infant in a sling over her shoulder.

"Follow me," the old man says, as he jumps in the truck with Dee.

Russ starts the Rover's engine. The woman runs up and hangs onto the door where I sit. Without looking at her Russ asks what she wants. "A ride to Nita'."

"Tell her we are not going to Nita'," he says.

I do, and reluctantly she steps back from the vehicle. "Why wouldn't you take her?" I ask. "She only wanted a ride."

We drive to Nita', Dee in the lead with the old man. An enormous Turkish fort comes into view, sand piling up against the walls in high drifts. The round towers are similar to those at Qaryat al Ulya. We stop east of the fort on the fringes of the village, in the green cluster of *athl* trees.

"Wait here!" our escort commands. He disappears up the dusty road to the town.

The usual collection of village children runs out for a look at us. Little girls peep between the dresses of their sisters—small, shy, equally curious, dressed in shimmering metallic cloth under the long, black, gold trimmed head scarves that frame their faces. First schools for girls are under construction in the Eastern Province, blue and white buildings with high walls or a link fence lined with palm mats to hide the view from the street of girls at play. Their

The Amir of Nita' 's family
greets us with laughter, as the
ladies toss their veils aside and
the little courtyard
acknowledges one world.

life follows the traditions of Islam, that's why Russ
was reluctant to give the woman a ride.

It is not the old shepherd who returns, but a tall
man in *bisht* (cloak) and crisp white *ghutrah*,
accompanied by a retinue of followers. The Amir of
Nita' invites us to the Amara (the Amir's offices) for
refreshment and rest. The man has come to
accompany us.

The Amara is of the same dun colored brick as
the rest of the town, distinguished only by a double
storey, a roof deck and a broad arched
entranceway. Veiled heads peek around doorways,
as we approach. Flashes of brilliant gowns color a
bare courtyard. A hand pushes a shutter open from
a grilled window and waves, wrist a jingle with
bracelets. Men and boys crowd the sandy roadway,
as the car stops, and we emerge. Word travels
quickly.

Inside the building we are separated: Russ and

Dee to the *majlis* where the Amir awaits. He invites
the men to relax on the rich carpets and cushions
against the wall. Then, with a flourish that swings
his sheer woollen *bisht* about him, he escorts the
girls and me down dark hallways to an inner
courtyard surrounded by rough brick walls. A well
stands in the center with rope and bucket ready to
be lowered. A protective roof of palm logs and fronds
forms a loggia, through which the breeze blows
relief from the hot afternoon.

Lined against the wall stand the women of the
hareem: the aunts, cousins, wives and daughters of
the Amir. The older remain erect and dignified,
while the young ones fidget and giggle. The bright
purple, green and gold of their gowns contrast with
the heavy veils that cover their heads. In this
meeting of the elite of Nita' with foreigners from the
west there arises a block between peoples. Locked
out by the black masks, the west retreats.

The Amir speaks. A tympani of ringing bracelets,

hair bells and high pitched chatter brings down the veils that are tossed aside. The little courtyard acknowledges one world. Time and place flee before gracious hospitality, as the dominant lady of the *hareem* beckons us to sit with her in the loggia. Satisfied, the Amir rejoins his male guests.

A long look at each other, as two cultures tread open ground, then the inevitable rush of curiosity. Are these your daughters? Is this one married? Where are your sons? How far is America? And, from us: Are you Ajmi? Have you been to Riyadh? How old is the baby? Busy black women, the stamp of Africa on their features, spread fresh fruits and plump dates on palm mats along with chocolates and sugary sweets, then serve tea in tiny glasses. With their skirts and cloths they swish flies that cling in the hot and heavy air. It is humid in the courtyard, and the gathering of clouds threatens deeper discomfort.

An infant yells. His mother unlocks her legs where she squats and takes him to the well. Setting the child in the bucket, she dips him into the cool depths. The child's body glistens with the water, as she returns to the group and rocks him to sleep on her lap. Brushing back the baby's damp hair, she lays a comforting hand on his belly. We smile at the magic of her simple wisdom. No pampered infant— just human response to human need.

It is too soon when the Amir returns to escort us back to the cars. Our visit must be short, for many tribesmen will come and pay their respects to the Amir. It is sufficient that we have paused here briefly, leaving behind our promise to return.

The wide, flowering valley of Wadi al Miyah undulates with vast camel herds. Groups cluster about several wells. "*Umm Jamal*" mother of camels, the wells of the Valley of Waters.

"There's a black one!" Cyndy shouts.

I'd almost forgotten Qaryat al Ulya and the sacred herd of the Mutair. Faisal's warning comes back to me: "Don't ask any more. It's political."

Rough ground ahead, and a tire blows. Russ and Dee wrestle with the second spare. The escarpments are now at our backs, collecting straggling bands of clouds. A grey pall settles between the land and the sky. Day begins to close before its time, diffusing familiar landmarks in a deepening mist. We have come this way on many excursions and know what lies ahead: patches of deep sand, deposits of large rocks, beds of rough limestone.

A new element slows us down—the spattering of raindrops that coagulates the dust on the windshield. Penetrating the mist ahead, our headlights beam on a barrier. Six closely wrapped Bedouins stand in a line across our trail, four with rifles pointed at the cars. Near the men stands a four-wheeled drive vehicle—a Toyota pickup, engine stopped.

One of the men passes by Dee's truck and approaches the Land Rover. He circles it, as a tent dog might sniff out a transgressor. The man wears trousers and a jacket, a bandolier across his chest and an insignia on his lapel. No Mohammed seeking water, but an official—military or police! At night, through the rain, the gun barrels are ominous. After a thorough investigation of the car, the man speaks to Russ.

"Get in the back, El," Russ tells me. "The man is riding with us."

A gunman rides in the truck with Dee, and in grim silence we drive off. No one speaks—no one dare! At the end of endlessness, the flares of the Abu Hadriyah GOSP spread like fire through the damp night. We turn north on the Northern Access Road— toward An Nu'ayriyah, not south and Ras Tanura. Ahead on the left appears the sharp glow of a campfire. We take off into the sand and stop near a tent. Russ and Dee disappear under the overhang, as the Bedouins direct them inside.

Couched camels face the tent. Sheep huddle behind the fire. Donkeys nudge to get an ear under the roof. A shepherd looks up from where he sits at the campfire, then pulls his cloak closer about him. As we wait in anxiety and silence, the ghosts of the Ash Shurf wander in the night wind, like wisps of smoke from the campfire.

Russ returns and starts up the motor.

"We can go home?" I ask.

"Why not?" he says.

"You were so long—I thought . . ."

"The inevitable coffee and hospitality!"

"Then—they are not Mutair?" I say, relieved.

Russ smiles. "So, that's what you thought! No, just police officials of As Sarar. They blew a tire and were looking for a replacement. When the officer realized our tires wouldn't fit, he asked to be driven to the tents of his brother."

"You mean—he would have swiped our tires!" I am more angry than if they had been Mutair.

Russ smiles. "We'll never know, will we?"

PART VII
"Ahlan Wa Sahlan!" (June 1964)

COFFEE—SYMBOL OF BEDOUIN HOSPITALITY
Get ready, my friend, it is coffee time,
Let the aroma of the roasted coffee
Spread all around.
Beware of half-roasted coffee
As well as the over-roasted one.
Roasting coffee needs patience,
And also needs care.
Watch for the time when
Coffee appears like diamond
In color, giving away a pleasant
Fragrance. That is the time
When you should start
Grinding it with rhythmic strokes,
Sending a shudder of delight in
Coffee lovers' hearts.

Serve and drink the wine-like coffee
In beautiful china cups
And have everyone become intoxicated.
Nothing would taste better, when the
Coffee is over, than your darling's lips.

May brings first warnings of summer. Sudden storms lay veils of fine dust, and brisk breezes from the Gulf whip white caps to a frothy foam. Skies glare a monotonous blue, and oasis palms lean, swollen with hands of first dates.

In the desert the *sabkhah* shrinks, cracked and dry. The soft grey *arfaj* of spring browns crisp and brittle. The fat *dabb*, giant lizard of the desert, turns from green to yellow. A painful dryness slowly bakes man, beast and land.

Still the Bedouin builds his *bait*, refusing to give up the last joys of freedom. His flocks seek meager food. The women's daily tasks take longer to finish. Men ponder on the day they must move to a settled area for summer camping with the tribe. In the *bait ash sha'ar* blowing dust covers waterskins, dropped *ruwaaq* (curtains), and camel saddles. Impregnated with sand, the long roofs sag. Sprinklings of yellow color black masks, bedding and cooking bowls. May also brings our last chance to go in search of the *bait ash sha'ar*. Long months of vacation travel, then Linda's departure for a school in Switzerland urge us to risk the driving hazards of loose sand and the discomfort of extreme heat. We sign out at the Main Gate of Ras Tanura, six o'clock on a clear Friday morning. The sun is already well up and

beats on the land. A palm tree, encroached on by a sand mountain, offers thin early morning shade. A stop for coffee—not for the need of food or from weariness, but to nourish the soul! Today there is no wind, and the desert is treacherous—a *jinn* that may suffocate with dust and heat.

Against hill and ridge, beside brackish well, or nestled in the folds of dunes we will find the long goathair roofs of black.

"Ahlan wa sahlan—welcome!"

"In the name of Allah, the Compassionate, the Merciful . . ." Khalid bin Jum'ah chants with reverence, his fingers floating above the words written in the book he balances on his knees. The *ghutrah*, thrown back, reveals close cropped hair, for Khalid works in the shops of the oil company and long hair may get caught in machinery. His new skills earn money that purchases clothes and food for the family. No longer need he depend on the largesse of his King, nor his wife wait outside the Amara walls for a share of daily meals distributed

Khalid sits in the *majlis* of his desert home reading to his young son, even though the twentieth century rushes him through years he has never lived.

We encounter our friend
Gordon Matthews along the
way and pause for an early
morning refreshment break.

by the Amir.

Khalid answered the call to change from idleness
to industry. His father responded to a different voice
—the cry of battle. Now the son owns a transistor
radio that brings the world and its events close to
his *bait*. Gone is the need to hail a passing caravan:
"What is the news of where you are from?" The
twentieth century has found Khalid. It rushes him
through years of growth he has never lived. The
concept of desert hospitality lives deep within him,
and he invites us to share coffee in the *majlis*. Our
presence calls to him, even as we listen to his desert:
"Come, Khalid, be as we are—you will see how easy
it is. No matter that you do not always understand
how you got there."

Khalid's young son, Hamid, stands quietly, as
his father reads the words of the Prophet. Listening,
the boy absorbs a storehouse of learning, love for
his family and peace for his soul.

"There is no god but Allah," Hamid recites.

During the hours of daily lessons from the Koran,
Hamid learns the course of his life and will reaffirm
his faith in the five daily prayers to be commenced at
the age of ten years. Outside the *qata*, the family
women listen to the words they will repeat to the
daughters in between daily tasks.

The coffee box stands by the cold fire, and Russ
sits and listens. One does not interrupt the word of
God.

Khalid closes the book and sets it in a box. "Fuel
for the fire!" he calls over the *qata*. Skirts rustle and
feet scamper, as the women dash into the *mahram*
and search out the sack of dung.

Beyond Khalid's *bait*, a pyramid of stones rises at
the edge of a dirt road. "Three drums of water,
please," the stones tell the red water truck when it
passes by. We read the stones, too. They told us
tents were built somewhere behind the dunes.

158

Young lambs and goats, loops
of soft wool about their necks,
escape the heat in the coolness
of the *bait*.

The young goats and sheep escape the hot sun in the coolness of the tent; a cocky little hen struts around them. The women of the *bait* have a new pet—not soft and responsive like the disgruntled camel or the loving *saluqi*. The chicken is sharp, crotchety and noisy, but the fruit of its body is good to eat. Allah has again provided for his children: clean water that does not have to be raised from a well, and eggs to add nourishment to a meal.

Khalid's wife welcomes me with eagerness: *"Ahlan! Ahlan!"* With a nudge and a sharp command, she orders the oldest daughter to chase the chicken from the tent. She, herself, shakes the mat for us to sit on, then draws her skirts about her and squats on the sand. Across the space of years we look at each other—Umm Ibrahim, named for the oldest son, and I: so akin, so eager, so full of questions that charge the air between.

"My daughter Linda is twelve years old," I say.

Umm Ibrahim acknowledges without understanding. Her Hijra calendar has eleven less days than ours and records 1384—not the Gregorian 1964. Statistics do not matter, for ours is a relationship between people. Linda and the oldest daughter Sarah appear to be the same age. The second daughter Aysha wears the traditional *bukhnuq* of young girls. Then follow Alia and Nahd.

Umm Ibrahim orders the oldest son to bring the goatskin into the *bait*. She stirs the coals and sets a tea kettle on the stones to heat, blowing the fire with leather bellows, ornate with chips of colored glass. Ibrahim watches, as Sarah struggles to remove the plastic wrap from a tin of Danish cookies we have brought. He dives, grabs the tin from Sarah's hands and dashes out of the tent.

The desert *ghazu* begins all over again—girls battle the boys. Umm Ibrahim shouts louder than the rest—no booty until the spoils are brought to her

159

Across the space of years we
look at each other—Umm
Ibrahim and I—as Aysha
brings her little sister to sit on
the mat.

for sharing. A submissive Ibrahim, followed by numerous brother and cousin warriors, returns the tin to his mother. Peace reigns, and later the goodies will be divided. Now is the time for tea.

The confusion has aroused a sleeping child. Through the dimness of the tent, I see a cradle of palm spines and a small girl trying to sit up. Wide-eyed, uncertain, the little one stares at us, as Aysha brings her to sit on the mat. Umm Ibrahim serves tea.

"This is Mash'al," she says. "The last of my children. I have nine."

She does not shrink from the numbers, but recalls them with pride—many sons and daughters make her husband a rich man. Besides, it is she who shares his greatest pleasure in all life's hardships—the coupling of husband and wife. She smiles and tells me they "bump" as often as they can.

"Dates!" Khalid shouts.

Sarah and Aysha scurry, their skirts stirring the sand. Aysha unties the goatskin of packed dates, works her fingers down through the neck, stretching it as she goes. The legs of the skin jerk convulsively with each thrust, and soon a sticky mass piles up on a metal tray. Alia, being younger, hurries the food into the *majlis*.

Umm Ibrahim raises the child from the mat and sets her on her feet. "*Shuf*," she says (look), calling my attention to Mash'al.

The piquant little face turns toward mine, the eyes studying me with the deep seated innocence of all wild creatures. A bit of lace trims her dress, and she wears a large amulet about her neck. How endearing a child!

Aysha seems to read my thoughts. "Look at her," she says. "Have you ever seen a sister as beautiful as Mash'al? How lucky I am to have such a sister!"

My extended arms invite Mash'al to come. The mother shakes her head and releases her hands that support the child. For a second Mash'al wavers, teeters uncertainly, arms seeking a balance, as the legs crumple and she falls in a heap on the ground.

"You see!" the mother cries. "She cannot stand. She cannot walk. It is the evil spirit!"

"Impossible!" I want to exclaim, but keep silent. How do I know all that the centuries have borne? The straight, plump legs are well formed. They should walk, but they do not. The muscles are liquid as water. "You must take her to the doctor—to the Clinic in Hufuf," I say.

"No," says Umm Ibrahim. "Mash'al did walk—but her beauty angered the evil eye."

How can I explain to her what lies beyond these worsted walls, of the great hospitals dedicated to helping children walk. Umm Ibrahim's knowledge extends no farther than the grasses and the sand—the Bedouin's acceptance of his fate.

"Yes, Aysha, your little sister is beautiful. Let's give her something special—a picture, just for her!"

Umm Ibrahim takes my enthusiasm and creates for herself a moment of triumph. There is more than just a picture between us—something good, even if it never comes back to her. Eagerly, she sets the child aright, straightens the skirt, the tilt of the cap, then arranges the legs, giving life to muscles that cannot move of themselves.

Pinpointed through the lens, I receive a transmission of her confidence—a willingness to test my values against her ancient ones. She will succeed, where I must fail: the *mahram* holds no light to record an image on the film. It is dark within the *bait ash sha'ar*, dark as the expectant eyes intent on me.

Alone on the mat, the center of attention, Mash'al begins to pout. Instantly, love creeps in, as Alia slips in to sit on one side of her sister and Aysha on the other.

The rear *ruwaaq* ripples where it dips from the roof, and for one brief moment a shaft of sunlight illuminates the serene face.

Who can explain the force of love that lights the world, or the stirring of a worsted wall where there was no breeze? Something beyond human control has responded to us both—perhaps even a promise that Mash'al shall walk again.

It is not the photograph, but the reaching out to touch each other that brings a burst of happy laughter. Sarah shakes the sand from a half-buried incense burner, painted red and decorated with brass nails and chips of glass. A piece of charcoal and a shaving of perfumed wood from India emit a light, curling smoke that carries the sensual fragrance of *ud*—burned on special occasions. Umm Ibrahim takes the brazier. She raises her long *burqah* (mask) and draws the smoke under the cloth to her face. So must I waft the intoxicating fumes toward my face and arms. The curling smoke stroking the skin is refreshing on a hot day.

The mother sets the burner on the sandy floor. She fans the charcoal with her skirt to increase the

161

As we head for the car,
Ibrahim rounds up an offender
and holds it out for us to see.

The rear curtain of the *bait*
ripples, and a shaft of sunlight
illuminates Mash'al's serene
face.

burning and augment the vapors, then lifting her
skirt, extends her legs directly over it. The scented
smoke circulates under the clothes to her body,
tantalizing as the stealth of fingers. Umm Ibrahim
looks at me with meaning, deep satisfaction
brightening her eyes. My skirt is short, but I must do
the same.

"The husband enjoys the *ud*, too," she says. Her
eyes sparkle in anticipation. It is not Khalid alone
who enriches the *bait* with children.

Umm Ibrahim pours more tea but is interrupted
by a shower of sand from the roof. Startled, I jump
up, and all rush out to see what happened, forgetful
of Mash'al, as she attempts to drag herself through
the sand.

Goats! Of course! Goats on the roof—I should
have guessed.

The *majlis*, too, has been disturbed by the shower
of sand, and Russ signals me away from the women.

"Been wondering when you'd come out," he
says. "Are you ready to go? Been drowning in
coffee!" Poor, patient Russ.

I round up the girls and we head for the car.
Above the chatter and profuse goodbyes rises the
cackle of a hen. Umm Ibrahim takes off, and as
quickly returns. "For you," she says, depositing in
my hand a warm, newly laid egg—speckled with
sand. It is not the egg I accept, but her
acknowledgment of a denominator common to
us both.

I turn to Khalid. "You must take your daughter
to the Clinic."

His smile is benign. "My wife does not believe in
doctors. But don't worry—there is time—it will not
run away." .

But—what of tomorrow? Mash'al's tomorrow?

The Rover jolts through *dikakah* terrain, as
though being torn apart. Time and again we are
thrown against the sides and roof of the car. The
apparently flat ground rolls with natural curves and
flood eroded washouts—undetected until the Rover
suddenly drops the height of a car. Arising from
such a spine-crushing drop, we see a man hurrying
across the desert, wildly waving his arms. Could he
mean us? We wait for him to catch up.

"Has the 'Id started?" he shouts, out of breath.
Russ tells him yes—yesterday: the 'Id al Adha, holy
days of the Muslim calendar that follow seventy
days after Ramadan.

"There's a tent farther on," Russ says. "This man
was sent to bring us there."

"Us—why?"

"You know the desert grapevine—and our dust
cloud . . ."

"Well," I say. "It won't be the first time we've
followed a Bedouin!"

Three black tents appear near the horizon—thin
lines suspended above a shimmering golden sea.
We do not pause at the traditional distance from
tents, but are directed to the *majlis* of the first one.
A man hurries out. Arms extended, his voice carries
across the desert.

"*Ahlan wa sahlan!*" Welcome!

I am caught in a tight embrace. What enthusiasm
is this that ignores the code of privacy?

"*Ahlan—ahlan!*" Welcome! Welcome!

Those twinkling eyes—that wiry beard—that
throaty laugh—those missing teeth! It is
Mohammed—the sly one—the happy family of the
Darb al Kunhuri! I am excited in turn—and
impressed, for it is I Mohammed escorts into the
majlis, for whom he fluffs up the sheepskin on the
camel saddle, and to whom he offers the seat of
honor!

"I don't believe it," Russ says. "Out of this great
expanse we've found Mohammed again."

"No," Linda says. "He found us."

The rush of questions won't stop. Where is Fahd—
the children—the new baby? All here, Mohammed

Goats on the roof! I should
have guessed what caused the
shower of sand in my tea!

The shower of sand has
emptied the *majlis* of men, but
the coffee fire still smoulders.

tells us.

"And Ya Baahah?" Cyndy asks.

Mohammed laughs, as he pats his belly.
"*Qahwah!*—Coffee!" he calls to the women.

At the edge of the roof's shade, Mohammed
scoops a shallow bowl in the sand. With twigs of
arfaj and rounds of dung he lays a fire. The dry twigs
ignite and a brilliant flame teases the dense fuel to
catch the heat. Three shining pots come from the
coffee box to rim the fire. He picks up a blackened
pot, transfers a little of its contents into a new pot,
then pours the residue of stock into the ground.
This time the coffee will be made fresh, with only a
little of the leftover to add a special flavor.

"*Miyah*—water!" he shouts to the women.

Dee beats Russ to his feet and heads for the truck.
We can't help laughing when Dee returns, for
yesterday is still here, and with it a can of sweet
water.

The *qata* falls in slings from pole to pole. I cannot
penetrate that embroidered curtain, but I know the
women are on the other side. I long to greet them—
to see if they are all there, but I know better than to
breach tradition. First coffee with Mohammed—
then the *mahram*.

Mohammed busies himself about the fire. From
time to time he glances at each one of us, repeating:
"*Ahlan—ahlan.*" He plunges the long handles of the
bean roaster and rake into the sand to keep dust
from the bowl he has carefully wiped. His shout
could invite the tribe—for isn't this the greatest of

days?—as he calls for sugar and beans, kept on the
women's side.

"How is your little granddaughter Samira?" I
ask, remembering the pale child with the infected
eyes. "And her mother, Amsha. Did she have her
baby?"

"All *zain*—fine—praise be to God."

Cyndy watches the antics of a dung beetle,
patiently rolling its huge cargo backwards to a
haven for burying. She squints through the bright
sunlight beyond the shade of the roof, for something
else catches her attention.

"Mom—look," she says.

A fleeting glimpse of faded print dress and a
child's departing bare feet. "Samira!" Time and
again she peeks around the *qata*, only to disappear
when I call her name.

"How she has grown," I say. "So plump and
healthy. How is your wife—and all Fahd's
children?"

"*Zain*—all good," he says.

I have spoken of family members in the presence
of Dee and Russ, and Mohammed has answered.
We are not strangers any more.

A woman ducks under the roof and deposits a
sack near the fire. She rushes to Cyndy and Linda,
kissing them on each cheek, and crooning as
though they were her own. Who else, but Umm
Fahd, the mother of Fahd and Mohammed's wife.
She comes to where I sit, hikes up her skirt and
squats directly facing me. She wipes her hands over

165

Time and again Samira peeks
around the curtain to stare
at us.

Water boils in the pot. Mohammed drops a
handful of green coffee beans into the black roaster
and holds it over the coals. The long handle enables
him to sit back from the heat. With the rake he stirs
the tender beans to heat them on all sides. The beans
begin to shiver, to dance excitedly within the bowl,
as they darken in color.

I kneel close to Mohammed, Hasselblad in hand,
to capture this special ceremony on film. He will not
allow it. This greeting is between friends, not for the
eyes of the camera that will steal some of it for itself.
A fragile moment, this. A miracle of reunion—
emotional satisfaction that belongs to the soul
through the generosity of Allah. Piece by piece, the
heart of Arabia has become mine. The once
insurmountable years are of no consequence. We
are together. Isn't that enough? You and I—the
whole of God's desert—a cup of coffee. All else
contaminates the purity.

Mohammed drops the rake and nearly tips the
roaster of browning beans into the fire. He dives to
retrieve a bean that has popped from the heat into
the sand. He tosses the hot bean to Cyndy, for those
that leave the fire, nutty flavored and crisp, belong
to the children.

A small wooden slipper receives the beans to cool.
The water pot is set back onto the coals. With a well-
worn cloth Mohammed polishes the mortar and
pours the roasted beans into it. The pestle rings
against the brass sides, as he pulverizes the beans.
Now and again he knocks off the powder that sticks
to the end of the pestle by striking it against the
mortar with a musical, dancing beat. The song of
fresh coffee rings through the camp, inviting all who
hear to join the coffee circle. Two of Fahd's sons
come running, begging to try their hand at ringing
the golden rhythm. The tent neighbor has heard
and comes swinging toward Mohammed's *bait*, his
step in rhythm with the song of the pestle. He waves
a camel stick to the beat and carries a child in his
other arm.

Into the bubbling pot go the pounded beans, then
a finger's pinch of cardamom, shell and all, are
broken up in the mortar. The froth of brewing coffee
rises and is poured into a second pot with the
cardamom. Three times the coffee froths and
changes pots, until finally it goes into the pouring
pot to settle. Fahd's son Abdullah reaches for the
brass cylinder that contains the tiny cups, all neatly
tucked inside with a piece of checkered cloth. He

the cloth of her dress before reaching out to take
both my hands in hers. What joy of reunion! I can
never forget this woman who tangled with another
to uphold the honor of her family. Now she intends
to stay right where she is—looking at me.

Mohammed scolds her. Tells her to leave.

"She is my friend," I say. "I wish to talk with
her."

"No!" the word explodes. "The *majlis* is not for
women!"

The fine line of proper conduct in a Bedouin
household has been reached. Umm Fahd rises,
plants a quick kiss on my forehead, shakes the sand
from her skirt, and with dignity retreats behind
the *qata*.

The tent neighbor hears the
call to coffee and brings his
child to Mohammed's *bait*.

hands Mohammed a length of palm fiber to be
stuffed into the beaked spout as a strainer. And then
the scented liquid—that delight of every Bedouin
household—the ultimate offer of hospitality—the
honor bestowed on a guest—is served with a
flourish and handed first—to me!

At midday the shepherds arrive with their flocks
to cool and refresh themselves before returning to
the glare and heat of the grazing grounds. Umm
Fahd brings in a metal bowl without a glance at me.
She is intent on her woman's business, as she hands
the bowl, full of tangy soured milk, to the nearest
herder. One by one the newcomers partake, still the
bowl is not emptied. Umm Fahd adds the sandy
water in which coffee cups were rinsed to the

leftover milk. She presses her hand to her mask, the
better to see, and sets the bowl on the ground where
animals crowd to share the shade, and now the
milk.

Summer's arriving heat is too strong to remain on
the open desert all day. Twice during the long hours
of brilliance, the animals and shepherds will return
to rest under the shade of the *bait*. A breeze ruffles
the coats of the sheep, and a donkey turns its head
to catch the movement of air. Men settle into the
sand, drawing up a knee, and talk. A city cousin has
come to visit as well as the Americans, and a
challenge is declared: who can catch and mount a
camel fastest! Nobody wants to walk the distance to
the grazing grounds, so the men squeeze into the

167

At midday shepherds and
flocks arrive from the grazing
grounds to cool and refresh
themselves under the shade of
the roof.

Everybody must take a turn
riding the *naaqah*. Complaints
rumble as Linda sits astride
her back.

Land Rover, and bucking like a bronco in a rodeo,
the car disappears behind a rise of ground.

We hear them coming before they appear—three
female camels and a calf, hissing and groaning as
they run for the tents. The men tumble from the car
and give chase. Mohammed brings a *naaqah* (cow
camel) to her knees, as she belches threateningly.
She is in excellent condition, for all spring the herd
has pastured on tender *arfaj* and an abundance of
wild flowers. Her hump of fat is firm and upright.

As summer continues, it may become limp and flat,
for the reserve fat will be used up during periods
when food and water become scarce.

The city cousin wins the day, for he has not
forgotten how to milk a camel, and catches the calf
by grabbing a flying hoof. Once a Bedouin always a
Bedouin. The deadly fun of former years, the
winning that made a man a man, fans embers in
the childish games of peace.

The government of Al Saud is strong. Oil revenues

169

Cyndy hangs on, as the *naaqah* refuses to cooperate in the day's games.

are flowing in. The political influence of the tribes lives on, but the demand for camel caravans has shrunk, as has the market for sheep-butter, desert firewood and hand woven saddlebags. The country's need is agriculture, but few Bedouins are willing to tie themselves to a plot of land. Yet, men like Khalid bin Mansur return to the desert to taste freedom and to challenge the soul.

"*Shaay*!" Tea. Mohammed calls. His demand arouses the lethargy of the women sitting within the narrow strip of shade cast by the roof.

I have followed Samira into the *mahram* and sit with Mohammed's wife who holds Amsha's baby on her spread lap. At the cry of "*Shaay*!" she rises, passing the baby to me. The child is a boy— Mohammed—born at a government clinic. Amsha's cousin in Jubail took her there.

Jubail is a small seaport town with a dirt pier about thirty miles north of Ras Tanura. Amsha lived there last summer—in a house. She would like such a house for herself, and more of what her city cousin has—such as a bed for the baby, not the *hababah* (leather hammock) that hangs under the roof where the air is suffocating. Amsha's new dress is of green nylon printed with yellow roses. She has a settled look. She will encourage her man to live in the

170

The city cousin wins the
games and proves that once a
Bedouin always a Bedouin.

town—women are the force in the family, and she
is tired of living with wind, and sand, and sun.

Mohammed's wife turns from the intense glare
beyond the roof that obliterates the shadows of
brush and rock, even of the storage skin for water
just outside the tent. With an eternal weariness she
unties the neck of the goatskin that hangs on a
tripod. The curled rope jumps and bounces like a
released spring, as she pours water into a bowl. Not
long ago the bowl was of wood, carved out by hand
and studded with silver. They were heavy and the
wood dried and cracked. Now the metal ones are
lighter. They come from Japan.

Life has not changed for Mohammed's wife. She
is still *umm al aiyal*, mother of the family who directs
the life of the tent. She rises before dawn when the
shepherd calls the day's first prayer. She directs the
shepherds to loosen the bleating lambs from their
ties within the *bait*, so they can feed from their
mothers before the ewes go to graze. With her
daughters she prods the camels to rise, and the girls
catch the first urine to use as a fragrant hair wash.
As she rocks the skin of camel's milk for souring, she
sings a song of the desert to the rhythmic squeaking
of the rope. The first light of day flushes the sky, and
all that she sees is hers: the open land, endless sky,

171

God's peace and beauty, that give her courage to live above the weariness, the ache of eyes, the leathered skin, the work-worn high-veined hands . . .

Small Samira clings to her mother's skirts. She will have nothing to do with the stranger who tries to make friends. All women are mothers in the closeness of the *bait*, but I am not the same. Amsha's new dress drags the sand, as she revives the fire in a pit at the edge of the roof's shade. She fills the kettle from the bowl of water Mohammed's wife has poured and sets it on the stones. Squatting, she adds sticks of *arfaj* and fans the embers with her skirt.

Samira has found the brass cylinder and pours the tiny cups onto the sand. She nests them into a wobbly tower, but the sand runs away under the bottom one, and they all fall down. Amsha hides one in the pocket of her dress, and the hunt is on. While Samira searches, her mother opens the sack

that is stitched down the middle to form two compartments: one for tea, the other for sugar. There is discipline in the packing and storing of goods. She fills a tiny coffee cup half full of tea leaves, then pours boiling water over them. When the water within the cup begins to color, she pours it off into the sand. Three times she infuses the leaves and pours off the tea's bitterness, before adding them to the kettle with the sugar. Mohammed's wife locates the tea glasses among the stores and takes them into the *majlis*. The men will be served first. I am of the family, and I, too, will wait.

"How are Samira and little Mohammed?" I ask Amsha for the third time. One cannot ask too many times after the wellbeing of family members.

She tells me that Fahd's children are here and well, but that Fahd has gone to Jubail to participate in the Ardah, the national sword dance, with his cousins.

Left: On a visit to Jubail, Amsha brought back a bed of palm spines for her infant.

Umm Fahd releases the rope around the neck of the goatskin and with an eternal weariness pours water into a bowl.

Samira hangs onto her
mother, as Amsha sets the
kettle of water on the fire.

Umm Fahd and Amsha talk of
life in Jubail, as Samira plays
with the brass cylinder that
stores the coffee cups.

"Do you know Jubail?" she asks. I tell her
"Yes." That I like the sea and the dhows that come
in from fishing and pearling around the Gulf.

"I will live there," she says, and there is certainty
in her voice.

I become aware of young Farida peering at me
over the support rope. She wears no *bukhnuq*. It is
too hot. I follow her to Fahd's *bait*, where the boys
are playing a game of jumping off the *qash*. All the
curtains are pinned to the roof to shut out the glare
that intensifies the heat. A saffron blanket hangs
under the roof, forming an air space that keeps the
room cooler and shuts out the brilliant sun the
porous worsted cannot hide. Unnoticed, Hussa
blends into the dimness of the interior. No relief for
her from mask and veil, and every breath is sucked,
labored through the cloth. Now and again she raises
the mask away from her face and fans the damp

skin underneath.

The boys have had their hair clipped for the
summer. Only a small tuft remains above the
forehead. Why? "To catch them when they run off!"
Hussa laughs. Later I learn that strips of paper
bearing Koranic verses are sometimes tied to the
tufts during sleep.

"Did Fahd get married?" I ask Hussa.

"In Jubail he will ask for a wife," she says.

I study her eyes, but she turns away. "Will you
marry, Hussa?"

Her hands fly to her veil, as if afraid to reveal her
thoughts. "Amsha's aunt speaks for a friend who
wants to marry," she says. "He has lived in America.
No one pays the bride price—is that true?"

"Yes," I tell her. "But the man provides
everything for his wife—clothes, money, house . . ."

"But the bride price is mine. If he does not pay,

175

Left: I toss a handful of candy inside Hussa's trunk, and young hands dive for the treasure.

Cyndy teaches the boys to jump on one foot, and Samir laughs because he did it first.

I will have nothing in case of divorce. I must have it!" She turns toward me, almost desperate. "And, he says I shall be the only wife!"

"Oh, Hussa, that's how it is in America. Wouldn't you like that?"

"No! No! That's not fair! I would have to do all the work!"

The two youngest boys have dragged out Hussa's metal trunk. She unlocks it and Abdullah opens the lid. They have seen its contents many times, but it is always a new game. I toss a handful of candy inside, and young hands dive in search of the treasure. Salim finds a piece of string, and I show them how to make a cat's cradle. Who can jump the longest on one foot? Abdullah wins this game because he is the oldest. Samir laughs when he succeeds, whereas little Salim's two feet want to leave the ground at the same time!

In the *majlis,* a decision is made: go to Jubail and join in the Ardah for the holy 'Id. No one has a sword—not the Bedu anyway. These days only a few officials possess ceremonial swords. It doesn't matter, for the dance will be the same.

The seat collapses, as five men crowd into the back of the Rover. It's of small concern compared to the joy ahead. Jubail—nobody asks how far. It's just—over there. We drive to relatives camped a half kilometer distant and encourage more recruits. Later we stop to camp, for Russ will not drive the desert at night, even with Bedouin guides. Tribesmen elect to continue on foot.

Next day we pick up the Darb al Kunhuri, an old friend now. Through swirls of dust and violent heat, I visualize the small seaport of dun brick walls, Customs House and ragged pier buoyed up by sand bags and chunks of marl. On either side dhows lean, stranded on running sand by the tides. The narrow streets are barely wide enough for donkey carts and lined with high walls that hide small cabins with palm roofs.

The salt smell of the sea is more real than memory, and I realize we are leaving the open desert behind. Donkey carts race from hamlets fringing an extensive *sabkhah,* and camel riders increase in number. The trail across the *sabkhah* is packed down. No danger of getting stuck. About a year ago we met a family here—a mother and several girls. They were gathering a stalk resembling asparagus, thick and reddish in color. "*Tartut,*" the mother told

us. "When the flowers die off and the stalk dries, then it is *tartut.*" She told me the names of all the children and that I must visit her. I recall only Sifla, the oldest, standing open to the sun.

We churn across the orange-gold sands of the coastal dunes. Soon the mud tower comes in sight, built to protect the town's water well. A small caravan is stopped nearby, loading stores onto pack saddles. The hands that shuffle the knots are henna stained.

The market square of Jubail is crowded with camels, donkey carts and men in holiday attire. Women wearing masks of purple and gold metallic cloth, coins jingling across foreheads, flit from doorway to doorway. Today the rules are relaxed, and they emerge to watch the grace and skill of their men in the Ardah, traditional dance of warriors. The festivities will not start for several hours, so we drive back to the Bedu section of town.

Groups of children run toward an open area, a block up from the sea, where three boys are building a fire of dried palm fronds. Men carrying several flat drums set them on edge back from the flame that blazes into dense smoke. We park the car and get out to watch, followed by three little girls in lacey dresses and sequin trimmed veils. One of them tugs

177

A year ago we met a mother
and her children gathering
"tartut" near a *sabkhah*.

Top: On the outskirts of Jubail we encounter a small caravan, and a Bedu woman holds her child for a picture.

Bottom: Cyndy joins Manirah and her family of daughters. "Everybody outside for a picture of this happy day!"

at my skirt, then hurries to hide behind an older sister. Linda is sure she has seen the girl before.

More sticks build up the flame—the campfire of the Bedu that has come to the town. I am aware of the older girl watching us, and walk toward her. Russ intercepts. "The Ardah won't start here for an hour," he says.

"See those girls," I say. "They want us to follow them—why don't you bring up the rear."

We walk down a rutted street with high walls and stop in front of a brass studded door. It opens—and there stands Manirah, the woman of the *sabkhah* who collected *tartut* almost a year before!

"*Ahlan!*" she cries, kissing me on each cheek. Her laughing children gather round, hair neatly braided, new dresses colorful. "You came! You came!" Manirah repeats, leading us into the house.

The dirt floor is covered with mats and rugs, freshly swept. Embroidered pillows line the walls. Tall, slatted window openings with metal bars are recessed and angled to direct the breeze into the house. We sit on the floor and relax against the cushions. Manirah's excitement bubbles, and orders flow like blessings from her lips.

"Sifla, bring the cloth—Muna, get the date cake—Sarah, the box of candy! Nejela, go for Pepsi and Orangina—hurry!"

A grab for a veil, and Nejela is out of the door. Fruits and sweets are set before us. Manirah brings paper napkins and knives, polishing each blade with a sheet of paper toweling. Then, with a determined gesture, she tosses aside her heavy face veil.

"See how happy she is," her husband Hassan says. "She is happy because you came."

There is an urgency to Manirah's life that will not be held back. Pressing on us the cakes and sweets, she talks about her children, mostly girls. Sifla wants to be a teacher—Nejela, a nurse and work at the clinic. Sarah, Muna and Wafa are going to school. When they are old enough, father will teach them the English he has picked up from the Americans at the oil company training school. She is glad to live in the town after the hardships of Bedu life, and is determined her daughters shall have a better future. And the young man in the large photograph on the wall? That is Mohammed, the son, who is in Pakistan learning to become a merchant.

"Oh, Allah is good," she says. "You must come again and meet our son. Now—everybody outside for a picture of this happy day!" She picks up her veil, then drops it with a laugh.

It is Manirah and others like her who leave the camel and the *bait ash sha'ar* behind. Change is not because foreigners are here. We are merely the instruments that implement the foresight of Ibn Saud, and the continuing of his wisdom by his sons.

The drums resound above the town. We are caught up in their fever. Run! Run to the Bedu section—the singing is about to begin! Several small fires are burning, and men hold the drums close to the heat to tauten the skins. They test the sound with a thump to see how the tone is enriched. Small boys feed the fires, as they watch how the drums are held.

The participants gather, some with polished swords and gold braid, leftovers from days past, now worn with pride and dignity. They form two opposing lines, and the drummers take their place between them. Two men carry large barrel drums, held over the shoulder by ropes and beaten forcefully with a thick, short stick. Others pick up the heated tambourine drums to be played staccato with the

Top: Young boys feed the fires
and extend the drums to
temper the skins.

Bottom: A small boy
concentrates on listening to
the beat, for it is he who will
lead the dance tomorrow.

fingers and the hard base of the palm.

The drummers bend rhythmically, forward and back, stepping on one foot and then the other. They lean low to carry greater force into the stick. White *thaub* sway, *ghutrah* ripple. "Come! Come! We commence the Ardah!"

A small boy finds a long stick. He paces in front of the drummers, listening, then picks up the beat and waves his stick aloft. Concentration sobers his young face, as he listens to the history of the desert. He misses the beat, then tries again, for it is he who will lead the dance tomorrow.

The shoulders of the men touch, as they stand in line, swaying in unison. Step—touch—lean with the kneebend—step again. They raise swords or long sticks high in the air, or pass prayer beads through fingers, each line chanting in answer to the other. The rhythm of the drums is slow, hypnotic, guided by the chant. It increases in pace, as more men join the lines and take up the sway.

Peace upon you, oh people
Who crave to punish the aggressor!

The call to the desert spreads through Jubail's Bedu

181

Left: A venerable townsman in brown *bisht* joins the dancers.

Top: A Bedouin group beats its way through the narrow streets of Jubail.

Bottom: The drummers lean low to carry greater force into the stick.

A child's shimmering
dress adds color to the
festivities.

area. Clouds of shimmering dresses augment those
along the wall, and children chant, and shout, and
dance on their own. A man catches the hand of his
young son, and they both join the end of the line.

> To stand against those
> Who prove to be at fault . . .

A venerable figure in brown *bisht* holds his
ceremonial sword high. In sedate rhythm, he moves
around the drummers; sunlight glitters along the
blade, and voices rise to a high pitch. The drums
beat as though the skins would burst—it comes
from the soul, from the earth, from the galloping
of hundreds of camels abreast in *ghazu*.

> We, the natives of Oja,
> Boldly penetrate the rising smoke—

Now the crowd makes way for a second man, who
enters the dancing area. He pauses in front of a line
of singers, fervor as sharp as the edge of a sword.
He is the poet, the director of the dance. He composes
a verse for the men to chant, as he sings louder
than the rest.

> Moving forward to the wall of death . . .

The poet two-steps around to the second line of men,
instructing the chanters in a reply.

> Moving forward to the wall of death,
> For the foe hides there.

Back and forth the singing continues, one line
responding to the other, as the poet gives the next
verse. Small boys listen and imitate, stepping in the
footsteps of Ibn Saud, who led his warriors in chants
of nationalism, valor and the greatness of God.

Reverberations echo from drums in other parts of
the town, calling men to converge on the square.
A Bedouin group beats its way through the narrow
streets, followed by women and children whose
holiday dresses splash color along the roadway.

In the square, a large assemblage of townspeople
and villagers stands several circles deep about the
performers. Women sit in a truck bed, the better to
see over the heads of watchers, and little girls flit in
and out among the long cloaks. The sun,
descending, shoots rays of orange fire from the top
of a distant *jabal*, as men begin to slip from the lines,
exhausted. A short rest to heat the drums, and the
lines form again, fresh recruits bringing new vigor
to the chanting. The Ardah will go on half the night.

The poet enters the dance,
instructing the men in chants
to be sung.

The spirit of the Ardah extends
beyond Jubail to recall the
days of Ibn Saud and the
founding of a Kingdom.

A tall, dark-skinned man steps into the ring,
sword raised aloft. A deep scar runs across one
cheek, whitened by the intensity of his dance.

"That's Ahmed Hussein!" Russ says. "A famous
sword dancer and one of Ibn Saud's warriors!" Russ
had met him at festivities for the King in Dhahran in
1951, and again in Hufuf two years ago. We make
our way through the crowd to stand in the front
circle of watchers where Hussein takes up the dance.

The spirit of the Ardah reaches beyond the
seaport of Jubail. It becomes the future, even as it
recalls the past: the unification of tribes, and the
founding of a Kingdom—celebrated outside the walls
of old Riyadh with the poet, Ibn Saud, calling the
verses:

> We have fought with the sword,
> And with the sword we have conquered.
> Oh, my people, from this day forward
> We shall lead a new life.
>
> The sword we lay aside
> But never sheathe—
> Always ready to protect our rights
> When need arises . . .

EPILOGUE

A hot wind swept across the tarmac, as Lufthansa's Flight 681 from Frankfurt descended to the Dhahran Airport. The 707's wheels touched ground, stirring up the stagnant, salty smells of the Middle East. The plane taxied to a stop, and I felt the Hasselblad thump my chest as I descended the ramp. It was March of 1976 and I had come back to Arabia.

Russ had warned me of many changes taking place in the Kingdom, but on this night, all seemed the same: the long walk from plane to Customs, the scrutiny of men in *thaub*, the wet heat dampening enthusiasm for arrival, and the stars—jets of light spidering through slits in a worsted wall. The desert —when would I see it again?

Russ strained eagerly at the top of the stairs in the Custom's area. His tall frame towered above the mass of people searching the new arrivals. I waved. So did he. The gesture erased the enormous loneliness of four months separation.

"*Ahlan! Ahlan*—Mrs. Nicholson! You have come back!" a young Saudi called, as he hurried through the crowd.

"Yes, Yahya," I said. "And you didn't forget me."

The crush of western businessmen grabbing luggage put an end to further greetings. Yahya gathered up my bags, collected chalked curlicues from Customs officials and urged me through the final guard. The lobby throbbed with foreigners: Koreans, Thais, Indonesians, Celanese and Pakistanis—imported by the thousands and waiting to be transported to construction camp sites.

The world pounded on the door of Saudi Arabia, anxious and willing to effect the Second Five Year Plan for the economic buildup of the Kingdom. The peak of the oil boom had come and gone. Now a steady river of wealth flowed into the coffers of the government.

"You'll never recognize Al Khobar and Dammam," Russ said. "The Arabia you know has changed." There was a note of sadness in his voice.

We drove to Dammam on a wave of incorrigible traffic bent on suicide. New cars jammed the one lane roads, propelled by raw recruits eager to test the throttle. Wrecked cars writhed on rough shoulders, victims of the rush toward progress that lay on the roads. The *ghazu* warriors of old were back, strafing the roads in screeching automobiles. The ancient code of chivalry in conquest now gave way to indiscriminate maiming and death. Like myself, the silent desert watched in horror.

The streets of Dammam and Al Khobar lay trapped in construction rubble. Bulldozers exhumed the skeletons of ancient buildings, and mounds of fresh sand and gravel blocked thoroughfares. Broken sewage pipes, old and rusty, soaked their odors into the streets. Dislodged rats and scavenging cats rushed to keep ahead of heavy equipment cleaning up the towns.

Money buys anything, and Saudi Arabia had the money. Now the Kingdom purchased the experts of the world to implant their expertise on the ancient sands.

With the passing weeks and months following my arrival, I marveled at the rapid growth of the Eastern Province. The skyline changed daily. Old structures fell to tall apartment buildings with handsome facades. Enormous plush hotels rented rooms for $200 a day. Beautiful Arab homes clustered in compounds, their delicate pastels and lace tiles giving new dignity to the streets. Universities, hospitals and industrial plants filled empty spaces, all connected by broad boulevards lined with young trees. Sleek new shops stocked anything you wished to buy—at a price. These days of transition and bewilderment inched out a way of life that would not return.

Russ was right. The Arabia we had known existed only in small pockets, and in the hearts of conservative Muslims. What had happened to the quiet days with their time to live? The rickety chairs we sat on at Balooki's grocery when offered a Pepsi on a hot afternoon? The glass of sweet tea with Jamil in his incomparable, one and only, country store—where you could find anything from toothpicks to bird cages. Haste had found its way here—haste and modern machines, responding to a frenetic need to discover this land, to establish a competitive identity.

And what of the Bedu—the gracious hospitality of the *bait ash sha'ar*, the endless camel herds, the gentle women and children? I had to know for myself. On a clear Friday, Russ agreed to drive the Northern Access Road as far as Kilo 100.

"We'll have to stick to the blacktop," Russ said. The Chevvy Impala is low to the ground without the capability of the Land Rover. "Don't expect to find a *bait ash sha'ar*. They've all gone from here."

The once open landscape was cluttered with power sub-stations, quarries, chicken farms, storage and earth moving areas. Then, "Ash Sheikh", our big dune, dominated the horizon. The road still curved its shoulder. Leader of tribes! Guardian of the *dirrah*! Landmark for travelers! Bulldozers growled at its base. They gnawed at the majestic sweep of shoulders that rose in an arc of perfect symmetry to the knife edge of the crest. Only sand. Handiwork of time and the restlessness of nature. A perfect form, crumbling under the hand of man.

Along Fadhili road, we sat on the loose sand for a picnic lunch. I gazed longingly at the terrain we once drove over, knowing that the Bedu don't come here any more. I dawdled packing up the lunch. I couldn't believe that somewhere—as the sun sank lower—there wouldn't be a camel herd returning home. I could even smell it. Quickly, I crossed the road, plunged into soft sand and the open country that spread before me. Dotting the landscape in humped back regularity, a camel herd appeared, marching in and out of the centuries. Mothers and babies nibbled endlessly, swinging their awkward legs, grumbling their rumbling sounds, exuding their strong smell, sand singing its endless song through shuffling hooves.

A herder, relaxed on his tall mount, rode toward me, raising a camel stick in greeting. The wind toyed with my hair as if to say: "Didn't I tell you they were coming?"

I greeted him as of old: "God's peace upon you." Eagerly I asked after his children and his *bait*, and if he was Ajmi. He grinned, curious that I knew his country, accepting my explanation that I had visited his *dirrah* and his families.

"Then, you are Ajmi, too!" he said, the ultimate in generosity. He leaned closer to me. "You must come to my *bait*. I have babies. A new son—a lovely lamb—a black camel born just this morning. So small—so beautiful!"

"You still live here?" I said. "I thought the Bedu had all gone!"

"Gone? Where?" His look was puzzled. "This is my country—my home."

The lure of past days rose within me. At this moment I belonged to the desert—to laughing Muna of the rainpool, and to the strength of Umm Fahd. I caught the sun's flash on the green Chevvy, as Russ edged the car onto the road, the motor loud. I heard his unspoken words: precise—cold—factual. That life can never be the same as before.

The herder didn't notice: his eyes eager, smile inviting.

I yearned to go with him but stepped back—away from myself. "I cannot go," I said.

The Bedouin leaned closer. He cupped his hands. "So small—so beautiful." He tapped his mount and together they moved away.

Time, as measured by each generation in days and years had moved on. Nothing remains the same—except the desert itself: inhospitable, violent, free. The days of yesterday, of today—yes, those thousands of years past when first the nomad wandered are all stored amid the endless shifting of sand.

Even those days that were ours.

I crossed the road to the car. The wind took these moments and built them into never ending designs of peaks and valleys across the desert floor. It tugged at my skirt, urging me toward the distant specks of the camel herd blending into the haze.

And it brought voices—children's voices . . .

"Babies! Did you hear that, Cyn?"

"Yeah! Come on, Linda. I'm going to see!"

"Hurry, Dad."

"Mom—aren't you coming?"

Only I heard—who, remembering, relived. But I who respond to change, walked back into reality, entrusting my answer to the touch of the wind:

"Wait for me! I'm coming with you!"

190

GLOSSARY OF COLLOQUIAL ARABIC TERMS

aba	man's cloak
abayah	woman's black cloak
abayaat	plural of *abayah*
ahlan wa sahlan	welcome
aish	what
aish ismahu	what's its name
Ajman	Bedouin tribe of Eastern Saudi Arabia
Ajmi	a tribesman of the *Ajman*
al aiyal	the family
al abu	father
alhamdulillah	praise be to God
Allah	God
Allahu akbar	God the greatest
Allah yusallimuk	God give you his peace
al Murrah	Bedouin tribe of South Eastern Saudi Arabia
amir	governing official, prince
Aneyza	Bedouin tribe of Northern Saudi Arabia
Ardah	national dance of Saudi Arabia
arfaj	desert shrub, diet of camels
arousa	bride
ashrah	the number ten
Ash Shurf	herd of black camels of the Mutair tribe
as salaam alaikum	peace be upon you
athl	tree similar to a tamarisk
Awazim	Bedouin tribe of Eastern Saudi Arabia
ba'ad daqiqah	wait a minute
Bahrain	island in the Arabian Gulf
bait	house
bait ash sha'ar	black goathair tent of the Bedouin
baksheesh	tip, gift
baladna	our country
Bani Khalid	Bedouin tribe of Eastern Saudi Arabia
bass	enough, sufficient
Bedouin	a tribesman of the desert
Bedu	people of the desert
bint	girl
bint al amm	first cousin (f.)
bintik	your girl, your daughter
bisht	man's cloak
bukhnuq	head garment for a young girl
burqah	woman's face mask
bushut	plural of *bisht*
buyut	plural of *bait*
dabb	large desert lizard
Dahna	geographical feature, strip of red sand
dallah	large beaked coffee pot
darb	desert trail
Darb al Kunhuri	old caravan route
dhulul	female riding camel
dikakah	terrain of shrubs packed with sand
dirrah	Bedouin tribal territory
fi	there is
fiamanilkarim	in the security of the Generous One
fiamanillah	in the security of God, goodbye
floos	money
ghazu	Bedouin raid
ghutrah	man's headscarf
ghutar	plural of *ghutrah*
hababah	child's leather hammock
hadh	luck
hajj	pilgrimage
hamdh	salt bush
hareem	pertaining to women and their place of residence
haudh	basin, trough
hijra	settlement
hinaak	over there
ibn al amm	first cousin (m.)
'Id	holiday, holy day
Ikhwan	brotherhood
imsh	go, leave
inshallah	if it is the will of God
ithnain	the number two
jabal	mountain, butte
jallah	dung
jamil	beautiful (m.)
jarbu	desert rat
jareed	dried palm sticks
jerbah	goatskin waterbag
jibaal	plural of *jabal*
jihaaz	trousseau
jihad	holy war
jinn	a spirit

191

juss	cement-like building material		*riyal*	monetary unit of Saudi Arabia
			riyalaat	plural of *riyal*
kaif al hal	how are you		*ruwaaq*	curtain of a tent
kalaam	talk			
kam umrah	how old is he		*sabah al khair*	may the day attend you with goodness
khamsah	the number five			
kohl	black eye liner		*sabkhah*	salt flat common in Eastern Province
Koran	Holy Book of Islam			
kufiyah	man's colorful cap		*sabkhaat*	plural of *sabkhah*
kulla wahid	it's all the same		*saluqi*	Arab greyhound-like dog
			Saqlawi	a classification of horses
la	no		*shaay*	tea
laban	buttermilk		*shamal*	sand storm, wind from the north
laish	why			
lazam	must		*sharif*	noble (m.)
			sharifah	noble (f.)
ma assalamah	goodbye		*sheikh*	leader, honorary title
maghzal	spindle for twisting thread		*sheikhah*	feminine of *sheikh*, wife of a *sheikh*
mahram	women's area in tent			
majlis	a meeting, men's meeting or living room		*shuf*	look
			shukran	thank you
majnun	crazy			
maksar	woman's camel litter		*ta'aaliy*	come here (f.)
ma laish	it doesn't matter		*tafaddali*	make yourself comfortable (f.)
marhaba	hello		*tafaddalu*	make yourself comfortable (pl.)
marhabtain	reply to *marhaba*			
masaa' al khair	goodness attend you this afternoon		*tartut*	dried stem of a flower
			tawilah	old long coin of Al Hasa
minfadlak	please (m.)		*thaub*	an outer garment
miyah	water		*thiyaab*	plural of *thaub*
musabilah	Bedouin trip to town for supplies			
			ud	fragrant wood
Muslim	a follower of Islam		*ulema*	learned men
Mutair	Bedouin tribe of Central Saudi Arabia		*umm*	mother
			umm al aiyal	mother of the children
			ummi	my mother
na'am	yes			
naaqah	she camel		*wa alaikum as salaam*	peace be with you
qadi	a judge		*wadi*	river bed, valley
qahwah	coffee		*Wahhabi*	follower of Abdul Wahhab
qash	wall of the stores built against the *qata*		*wajid*	a lot, many
			wajid zain	very good
qasir	tent neighbor		*waladi*	my son
qata	dividing curtain in a tent		*wasm*	tribal marking
qataat	plural of *qata*			
			ya akhuiy	oh, my brother
rafiq	tribesman who guarantees safe passage		*yalla*	let's go
			yawmain	two days
risan	rope halter for a horse			
			zawjati	my wife